Relief from Insomnia

Relief
from
Insomnia

Getting the Sleep
of Your Dreams

Charles M. Morin, Ph.D.

DOUBLEDAY
New York London Toronto Sydney Auckland

A MAIN STREET BOOK
PUBLISHED BY DOUBLEDAY
a division of Bantam Doubleday Dell Publishing Group, Inc.
1540 Broadway, New York, New York 10036

MAIN STREET BOOKS, DOUBLEDAY, and the portrayal of a building with a tree are trademarks
of Doubleday, a division of Bantam Doubleday Dell Publishing Group, Inc.

Library of Congress Cataloging-in-Publication Data

Morin, Charles M.
Relief from insomnia: getting the sleep of your dreams / Charles M. Morin.
— 1st ed.
  p.   cm.
Includes index.
1. Insomnia—Popular works. I. Title.
RC548.M675   1995
616.8′498—dc20   95-42442
CIP

ISBN 0-385-47706-6
July 1996
First Edition

10   9   8   7   6   5   4   3   2   1

To my wife, Paule,
and my children, Geneviève and Sébastien

Acknowledgments

I am indebted to several hundred patients afflicted with insomnia for sharing their experiences with me and to many colleagues who have taught me a great deal over the years in treating this sleep disorder. I am thankful to the National Institute of Mental Health, which has provided financial support for my research program on insomnia since the beginning of my professional career. Special thanks to an esteemed colleague, Dr. Cheryl Colecchi, a clinical psychologist who has contributed drafts of three chapters and commented on several others. I also wish to thank my agent, Laura Blake, editor, Frances Jones, and copy editor, Frances Apt for their assistance in the production of this book. Finally, I am most grateful to my wife and children, for their support and understanding during the long days and short nights as I was writing this book.

Contents

Tables

Introduction

If you have trouble sleeping at night, chances are that you also have difficulties coping during the day. And you are not alone. Insomnia is one of the most common health complaints, with virtually everyone experiencing an occasional bout of insomnia and many more struggling with chronic sleep difficulties. Insomnia is not a trivial problem; it can adversely affect a person's life—causing emotional distress, fatigue, diminished productivity, as well as interfering with relationships and quality of life. Over the past 12 years studying and treating insomnia patients, I have been puzzled by two paradoxes. Although insomnia is a very common sleep disorder, very few people receive adequate treatment; and when a person decides to seek treatment, it is often only after months or even years of battling with sleepless nights.

All this leads to a great deal of unnecessary suffering, because insomnia is a highly treatable condition. However, many of those who suffer are discouraged by the lack of immediately available resources on sleep disorders, while others suffer in silence, as they don't feel comfortable talking to their doctors about sleep due to a general sense that insomnia is not perceived as a real health problem. When patients do consult their physicians, sleeping pills are often prescribed, although this is too frequently the only recommendation—and this does not address the underlying problem. Sleep experts agree that drugs should not be the first line of treatment, and most patients prefer not to use drugs. Recent clinical research has shown that insomnia can be effectively treated with relatively simple changes in lifestyle, behavior, and the attitudes that interfere with restful sleep. Many of the recommended treatment methods for insomnia can be easily implemented with minimal professional guidance. This self-help book was written with the idea that knowledge is often more powerful than a prescription, and as an informed consumer it is hoped that it will give you all the information needed to rediscover the pleasure of sleep.

Relief from Insomnia describes a step-by-step, drug-free, and clinically proven treatment program for insomnia. It is a self-help book that provides simple and practical methods to get a good night's sleep without drugs. Thus, the main focus is on psychological rather than pharmacological therapies. It is also a reference guide that provides practical information about normal sleep and many of its disorders other than insomnia.

The book is organized into three general sections. The first chapter presents an overview of sleep and answers key questions about the different types of sleep, why and how much sleep is needed, and how sleep patterns change as we grow older. The second chapter describes the different types of insomnia, their causes, symptoms, and consequences. Chapter 3 discusses several conditions for which you should seek professional help and details on what to expect when you sign up at a sleep clinic.

A complete self-management approach to overcoming insomnia is described in the second section. Each chapter covers a different angle of the problem, and describes helpful strategies to: change poor sleep habits; revise faulty beliefs and attitudes; learn relaxation skills to control daytime stress and bedtime worries; and make your bedroom environment more conducive to sleep. A discussion of the use of sleep medications, when they can help and when they should be avoided is also included, and a program for those who have become dependent on sleeping pills and wish to kick the habit is outlined.

In the last section, useful strategies to beat jet lag and to cope with shift work are described, as are several other sleep disorders such as sleep apnea, narcolepsy, nightmares, and many others. The main symptoms of these conditions are depicted in order to help you recognize those disorders and assess your need to seek professional help. In chapter 13, common sleep problems in children are reviewed, as are practical solutions for parents dealing with those difficulties. The last chapter outlines key strategies for maintaining healthy sleep patterns in late life. A list of professional organizations and support groups for patients with sleep disorders and their families is provided in an appendix.

Written in an easy-to-understand language, this book is intended for the general public. It will serve as a useful informational resource for you or a loved one about effective nondrug therapies for the management of insomnia. It will also be of interest to those who wish to learn more about sleep and the major symptoms of its many disorders. Although it is not intended to substitute for professional treatment, many people will find this guide provides sufficient information for them to overcome their insomnia problems, whereas others will find it useful to complement the treatment recommendations provided by health-care professionals.

CHARLES M. MORIN, PH.D.

1

The Facts
About Sleep

Getting a good night's sleep is for most people a wonderful and rejuve-
nating experience. It is analogous to taking a mini-vacation to replenish
your physical and psychological energy. You come back from the journey feeling revitalized, with a more positive outlook on life, and better
prepared to accomplish what's on the agenda for the day. When you
have plenty of sleep, you often take it for granted. Those who don't get
enough of it, however, may come to talk about it as someone does who
has been deprived of food, water, or sex.

If you have trouble sleeping at night, you're in good company. More
than one in three adults complain of insomnia, and many more suffer
in silence. Fortunately, the field of sleep disorders is rapidly evolving,
and new methods are now available to treat most sleep problems. I will
begin this book by reviewing some basic facts about the nature of
sleep, its types, functions, changes over the life span, and its relationship to our daytime activity, mood, and health. Since the main purpose
of this book is to learn practical solutions to insomnia, it makes sense
first to have some basic understanding of normal sleep.

The Passage from Wakefulness to Sleep

Sleep has long been a puzzle. For years, it was considered an inactive state during which the mind and body were completely shut off, disconnected from the outside world. Although it occupies about one third of our lives, only recently have scientists begun to explore its mysteries. Experts now agree that sleep is an altered state of consciousness, having a life of its own. Although it appears to be passive, it is, rather, an active condition, during which the mind and body functions continue, although in different modes, even in the absence of environmental stimulations. After you turn out the light and let your thoughts drift away, you enter a different world. Your eyelids close, your pupils shrink, breathing becomes slower, and heart rate and temperature drop. Your body enters a deep state of relaxation (the alpha state); your mind wanders, mixing odd images, thoughts, and monologues. This pleasant shift, from wakefulness to drowsiness to sleep, is called a hypnagogic state. It is often accompanied by a sudden muscle jerk and the impression of falling through space, hence the expression ''falling asleep.'' You lose consciousness for a time, but early in the night, anything can bring you back to consciousness—noise, light, the movements of a bed partner. The experience of falling asleep, like that of coming out of sleep in the morning, is a gradual process. There is no switch that just turns on and off. The pleasantness and duration of the transitional phase, from wakefulness to drowsiness to sleep, vary from person to person. If you are healthy, free from worry, and a good sleeper, this experience is usually fairly brief but pleasant. But if you are plagued with insomnia, you may undergo a long, agonizing, and frustrating ordeal.

Two Types of Sleep, Two Worlds Apart

Researchers have identified two types of sleep: rapid eye movement, or REM sleep; and non-REM, or NREM sleep. NREM sleep may be anything from dozing to a deep slumber and has four stages, each progressively deeper and each characterized by different brain-wave activity (see Figure 1.1). As you begin to doze and enter stage 1 sleep, your thoughts wander and you may drift in and out, experiencing a sensation like daydreaming. Your eye movements become slow and rolling, your breathing more even, and your muscles are more relaxed. Stage 1, often called light sleep, is a transitional phase, lasting only a few minutes, before you enter what is considered ''true'' sleep, stage 2. In this stage, brain-wave activity is characterized by sleep spindles and K-complexes (see Figure 1.1), a momentary brain-wave pattern characterized by a sharp negative deflection followed by a positive one. About 50 percent of each night is spent in stage 2 sleep. Stages 3–4, often grouped together, are regarded as the deepest and most restful sleep. Brain waves are deeper and slower. This is the period of slumber most difficult to rouse a person from, and there may be a short period of confusion following the awakening. Depending on a person's age, stages 3–4 sleep make up between 5 and 20 percent of total sleep time, but some nights you may not achieve it. Stages 3–4 sleep is also called slow-wave sleep or delta sleep, because brain waves are slower and of higher amplitude during this phase. NREM sleep is often described as ''an idling brain in a movable body''; our mind is quiet, but our bodily functions remain in their usual states, although in slower motion.

By contrast, during REM sleep there is considerable mental activity; our dreams originate in this phase, which occupies 20 to 25 percent of a typical night. Everybody dreams during REM sleep, even if she has no recollection of the dream the next day. Unless she wakes during or shortly after an episode of REM sleep, she is unlikely to remember the dream. Studies show that more than 85 percent of subjects awakened from REM sleep recollect a clear dream with a storylike progression; strong emotion is often present. REM imagery is very vivid, and sometimes bizarre, often incorporating colors and sounds. By contrast, less than 15 to 20 percent report dreaming when awakened from non-REM sleep, and the imagery usually involves a thought, a picture, or a situation incorporating elements of the immediate environment. In addition to dreams, several other changes accompany REM sleep. First, there are periodic bursts of rapid eye movements (which give this phase its name); the heart rate speeds up and becomes more variable; the blood pressure fluctuates; and both oxygen consumption and blood flow to the brain are higher than during wakefulness. Healthy males, from infancy to older age, experience penile erection during REM sleep, and

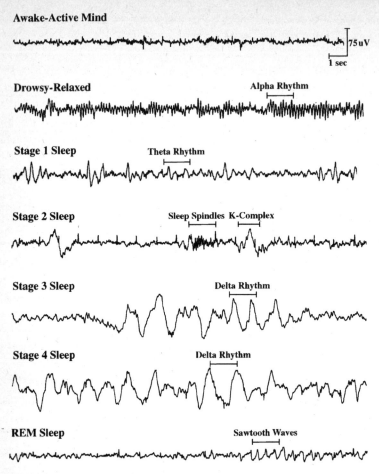

Figure 1.1. Brain-wave activity associated with alert wakefulness, relaxed wakefulness, and different sleep stages. Beta waves are associated with an alert state of mind. The alpha rhythm (8 to 12 cycles per second) is typical of a relaxed wakeful state (with the eyes closed) preceding the onset of sleep. Theta waves are characteristic of a light sleep, whereas the delta rhythm (0.5 to 2 cycles per second) is monitored during the deepest stages (3–4) of sleep.

females show engorgement of the clitoris. Interestingly, the ability to regulate body temperature is lost during REM sleep. Studies have shown that even with changes in ambient temperature, there is no sweating or shivering. And, strangely, the body is paralyzed, perhaps to prevent us from acting out our dreams. Aside from periodic muscle twitches, most voluntary movements are shut off. There are, however, numerous changes in body positions throughout the night, usually accompanying changes in sleep stages. Even when it seems that we fell asleep and woke up in the same position the next morning, we have probably changed position—and awakened—numerous times in the night without remembering that the next morning.

SLEEP CYCLES IN THE NIGHT

Each person's sleep pattern is unique, though the quality and duration vary with age, health, and lifestyle. The sequence with which we move from one stage to another, however, is fairly stable among good sleepers who maintain a regular sleep-wake schedule. During a typical night's sleep (as depicted in Figure 1.2), we alternate from one stage to another, often in cycles moving from light to a deeper sleep (stages 1–4 of non-REM sleep), followed by several minutes of vivid dreaming (REM sleep). Adults typically enter sleep through the non-REM stages, and the first REM period takes place between 70 and 90 minutes of falling asleep. On average we complete 5 cycles every night. REM sleep occurs in 4 to 5 episodes of increasing length and intensity throughout the night. The first period may last 15 to 20 minutes; the final one, in the early morning, is more intense and may last 30 to 60 minutes. The last third of the night is dominated by REM sleep, while most of the deep sleep (stages 3–4) takes places early in the night.

HOW MUCH SLEEP IS ENOUGH?

Individual sleep needs appear to be determined biologically, with age a significant factor. Newborn babies sleep on average 16 to 18 hours a day and toddlers around 10 to 12 hours at night and 1 to 2 hours during the day. By the time children reach nursery school age, their daytime napping is infrequent, and their nighttime sleep diminishes to 9 or 10

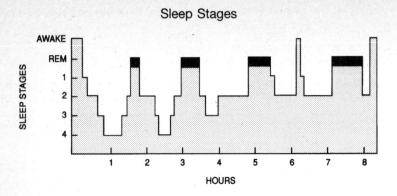

Figure 1.2. This figure (a sleep histogram) illustrates the typical night's sleep of a young adult who does not have sleep difficulties.

hours. Teenagers need about 9.5 hours of sleep to be most alert during the day, but they rarely get it. Young adults with no sleep complaints spend between 7 to 8.5 hours sleeping at night. Elderly people sleep on average 6.5 hours a night and may get an additional hour with an afternoon nap.

There is a widespread assumption that 8 hours of sleep is what every adult should aim for, but sleep needs vary widely, from as little as 4 or 6 hours to 9 or 10 hours per night. So if not everybody needs 8 hours of sleep each night, how do you determine what's best for you? The most important thing is to experiment with various sleep durations and then monitor how alert you are and how well you function the next day. If you feel drowsy or fall asleep at inappropriate times or places, you did not get the right amount of sleep the night before. A well-rested person usually will not fall asleep, even in a warm room, listening to a boring lecture after a heavy meal. The sleep-deprived person, however, will not only fall asleep under the same circumstances but may doze off during an important meeting or an interesting concert. Ideally, you should sleep for as long a period as you need to feel refreshed in the morning and alert throughout the day.

But, of course, most adults don't get the sleep they need. The majority, particularly young adults, get fewer than 8 hours of sleep on week nights, and many try to get by with 6 or 7 hours. The fact that the majority will exceed 8 hours on weekends is a clear sign that the week-night amount of sleep is insufficient. Although you may be able to function temporarily with less sleep than you require, eventually the lack will catch up with you; it's like trying to wear a shirt of medium size when you really need a large one. Many people who are chronically sleep-deprived accumulate a sleep debt during the week. Some are able to catch up on weekends, but many—with family responsibilities or a second job—can't afford the luxury. Even if the sleep deprivation is mild, an established pattern may significantly impair daytime functioning, mood, and alertness. We will return to the effects of sleep deprivation later in the chapter.

Sleep is an increasingly precious commodity. Over the last several decades we have reduced our nightly sleep by well over an hour per night. Surveys of sleep habits conducted in the early 1960s revealed that most people were reporting between 7 to 8.5 hours of sleep per night. Similar surveys done nowadays show that more than 50 percent report fewer than 7 hours of sleep on week nights. Not too long ago everything shut down at dusk; today, many people work a second job on evening or night shifts, stores and shops are open longer hours, and television programs are available almost 24 hours a day. This host of activities competes with sleep and possibly contributes to a chronic state of sleep deprivation.

CHANGES IN SLEEP PATTERNS OVER THE LIFE SPAN

Age is the single most important factor affecting the amount and quality of our sleep. We just saw that the average sleep time in a 24-hour period decreases from 16 to 18 hours during infancy to about 7 to 8.5 hours in young adulthood, and many older people may get no more than 6.5 hours. But with napping, a fairly common practice after retirement, the total amount of sleep in a 24-hour period remains fairly constant from middle age to late life. What seems to change with age is not so much the duration as the efficiency and quality of sleep. Older adults often spend more time in bed than younger people to get the same amount of sleep; with aging there is a decrease in deep sleep (stages 3–4) and a corresponding increase in light sleep (stage 1). The person sleeping more lightly is more likely to be awakened by noise or the movements of a bed partner, and this may explain why insomnia is a frequent complaint among older people.

The greatest changes in sleep patterns take place from infancy through adolescence, the period of numerous other developmental changes. There is a close connection between the amount of REM sleep and the speed of brain maturation. About 80 percent of a fetus's sleep is made up of REM, and infants spend about 50 percent of their sleep in REM. You can probably determine, even without special monitoring equipment, when your infant is in this sleep. In addition to the characteristic rapid eye movements, there are periodic facial twitches and smiles, and respiration is often irregular. The proportion of REM sleep gradually declines from 50 percent during infancy to about 35 percent at three years, through childhood and adolescence, and stabilizes in young adulthood. A 25-year-old spends about 20 to 25 percent of an 8-hour sleep episode in REM, and there may be a slight dip in this when the adult reaches his sixties or seventies.

Why We Need to Sleep

If a person is kept awake long enough, sleep will eventually override any desire or attempt to prolong wakefulness. You can probably relate to this if you have stayed up all night because of a sick child or an approaching deadline. A single night without sleep is enough to convince anyone that sleep is essential, a biological necessity comparable to the need for food, water, and sex. Exactly why we need to spend about a third of our lives asleep is still puzzling to many scientists. Some scientists believe sleep serves a protective function against predators at night; others think it preserves energy expenditure by lowering our metabolic rate. And to others, REM sleep is an unconscious outlet for repressed wishes, urges, fears, and frustrations. Although each of these theories is interesting, they are difficult to validate. Nonetheless, a great deal of what we know has come from sleep-deprivation studies, in which volunteers are monitored in a laboratory throughout the night. Every time they enter a particular stage of sleep, a technician on duty wakes them up with noise. As the night progresses, it becomes increasingly difficult to prevent someone from entering a specific stage of sleep; the subject becomes more irritable, and the technician's effort or noise intensity has to be intensified.

From these studies we have learned that when a person is deprived of a particular sleep stage, there is a natural rebound (or increase) of that kind of sleep during the recovery period. If on a given night a person is prevented from going into deep sleep (stages 3–4), he will spend more time in that type of sleep the next night. A similar phenomenon occurs with the sleep patterns of people using antidepressant medications. This class of drugs diminishes the amount of REM sleep; when a person stops using the medication, there is a temporary increase of that particular sleep stage, sometimes experienced as nightmares. These observations indicate that not just any sleep is necessary; we need all the different kinds of sleep in order to be healthy.

Other experiments have led researchers to conclude that NREM sleep is primarily involved in restoring physical energy, whereas REM sleep plays a more important role in learning and in problem-solving. The recuperative functions of NREM sleep are noted in two observations. First, a person deprived of stages 3–4 sleep is, the next morning, filled with complaints of aches, pain, and muscle stiffness. Second, regular aerobic exercise tends to increase the time spent in those deeper sleep stages. Together, these observations suggest the possible role of NREM sleep in restoring physical energy. Other studies suggest that REM sleep serves two important information-processing functions; first, in consolidating newly learned materials, and second, in maintaining psychological equilibrium. For example, an intensive course in learning a second language increases the amount of time spent in REM sleep. On the other hand, selective deprivation of REM sleep during this type of learning experience interferes with retention and memory consolidation of new materials. So these observations provide fairly convincing evidence that REM sleep plays an important role in processing, storing, and retrieving new information.

Psychotherapists have long been interested in dream analysis as a potential window to the unconscious. More recently, studies conducted by Dr. Rosalyn Cartwright, a clinical psychologist at Rush–Presbyterian–St. Luke's Medical Center in Chicago, have shed some light on the effect of our daytime experiences on REM sleep. She examined the dream contents of people undergoing divorce and discovered that the contents varied, according to whether the participants were depressed or coping well with the crisis. The dreams of depressed participants were more pessimistic, filled with a sense of guilt, inadequacy, and poor self-esteem; the participants who were coping well during the day also reported dreams that reflected more adaptive emotional responses to their new situation. The contents of their dreams suggested a greater sense of self-control and a more positive self-image. REM sleep apparently plays an important role not only in the processing of factual information, but in the processing of emotional material as well. Our dreams may incorporate the ups and downs of our daily experiences and perhaps reflect our current state of mind.

A BIOLOGICAL CLOCK REGULATING THE TIMING OF SLEEP

Although sleep is a behavior that occurs at fairly regular intervals across all species, its timing varies. Humans sleep mostly at night, but many species sleep primarily during the day, and dolphins have only half their brain asleep at any one time. All living organisms—humans, animals, and plants—function according to a regular rest-activity cycle. The length of this cycle in humans follows a fairly consistent circadian (about one day) rhythm. The timing of the sleep-wake cycle in humans is largely determined by the light-dark cycle, which itself is governed by the rotation of the earth over a 24-hour period.

Neuroscientists have identified a small structure in the brain that serves as a biological clock regulating the sleep-wake cycle. Only about the size of a pinhead, this bundle of more than 10,000 neurons is located in the hypothalamus, at the base of the brain. It serves as a "light gauge" in measuring the amount of daylight exposure and determines the timing of the sleep and wake episodes. Light enters the eye through the retina, and nerve signals carry this information to the hypothalamus. In blind people, the line of communication between daylight exposure and the sleep center is short-circuited, and blind people often show the most irregular sleep schedules, sometimes feeling sleepy at 7:00 P.M. and wide awake at 3:00 A.M. In addition to daylight exposure, other factors play an important role in regulating the periodicity of the sleep-wake cycle. Among those are the alarm clock, work schedules, mealtimes, and social contacts. These "time markers"

(Zeitgebers) serve as environmental cues to keep the organism or biological clock in synchrony with the outside world.

Numerous biological functions are closely related to the sleep-wake cycle and are thus governed by circadian periodicity. Melatonin, a natural hormone produced by the pineal gland, is released exclusively at night. Because of its higher concentration in sleep, a synthetic melatonin product has recently been introduced on the market as a natural sleeping pill. Unfortunately, as we will see in Chapter 11, it is still much too early to say whether this product is of any help in improving sleep. Growth hormone is released soon after a person enters stages 3–4 sleep; it is present in highest concentration in a developing child and, along with deep sleep, diminishes over the course of life. Of the various biological functions controlled by circadian rhythm principles, body temperature is one of the most consistent. It fluctuates by about two degrees Fahrenheit within a 24-hour period and is closely correlated with alertness. Lowest in the early morning hours (4:00 A.M.), it starts rising before the sleeper wakes up, peaks in early evening, and begins declining around 11:00 P.M. Alertness is maximum as the body temperature increases (in the morning), and sleepiness is greatest as it drops. For example, it is hardest to stay awake around 4:00 in the morning, although this goes unnoticed by most people, who are sleeping at that time. However, those working the "graveyard shift" are at much greater risk of falling asleep on the job or at the wheel during that particular period than at any other time of the night. Many road accidents involving truck drivers occur in the early morning hours, when the traffic is least dense but the propensity to fall asleep is highest. There is also a slight decline in temperature in midafternoon, often corresponding with the second prime time for falling asleep. This suggests that the postlunch dip in alertness is related to temperature change rather than to a full stomach.

Is There a Chemical Sleep Substance?

Aside from its necessity and cyclic nature, we still know very little about sleep and about the mechanisms controlling the cyclical alternations between wakefulness and sleep. Scientists have long speculated that a chemical substance accumulates in the brain during wakefulness;

the longer a person is awake, the greater the concentration of the substance. When enough of it has accumulated, according to the theory,
the urge to doze off becomes strong enough to induce sleep. With the
onset of sleep, this substance is gradually released or it disintegrates.
Not too far from this hypothesis is the work of Drs. Alan Hobson and
Robert McCarley, researchers at Harvard University. They have shown
that the concentration and activity levels of some brain neurochemicals
fluctuate from wakefulness to sleep, and from NREM to REM stages.
We have seen earlier that NREM sleep is quiet in relation to REM
sleep. Hobson and McCarley have found that some brain cells (neurons) are turned off and others turned on during wakefulness and
NREM and REM sleep. For example, neurotransmitters such as serotonin and norepinephrine are turned on (more active) in NREM sleep,
whereas acetylcholine, off during NREM sleep, becomes particularly
active during wakefulness and REM sleep. These neurotransmitters are
brain chemicals; their concentration or activity levels change with
alertness, sleep, mood.

SLEEP IN HEALTH AND IN SICKNESS

Sleep is very sensitive to physical and psychological ailments. Not
surprisingly, during periods of ill health or emotional turmoil, sleep is
often the first casualty. Almost all medical and psychological disorders
produce disruptions of sleep patterns. In turn, difficulty in sleeping can
aggravate the underlying medical or psychological problem and perhaps even interfere with recovery.

Sleep and Pain

Almost any medical condition producing pain is likely to interfere with
sleep at night. Acute pain from injury or chronic pain from, say, arthritis can disrupt a person's ability to fall asleep directly and to stay
asleep. After a poor night's sleep, pain is more intense and unpleasant,
and mood is often disturbed, making it even more difficult for the
person to cope with the medical problem. Naturally, negative emotions
during the day further aggravate sleep difficulties the next night.

Dr. Harvey Moldofsky, of the University of Toronto, has been studying the sleep patterns of patients afflicted with fibrositis, a condition characterized by musculoskeletal pain. After unrefreshing sleep at night, fibrositis patients wake in the morning with muscle stiffness and aches all over their bodies. They feel almost as if they had been run over, back and forth, while they were asleep. Their nights are characterized by a condition known as alpha-delta sleep. Alpha rhythms, the brain-wave pattern associated with relaxed wakefulness, typically occur just before the onset of sleep and are relatively infrequent thereafter in pain-free individuals. In pain sufferers, however, alpha brain waves may persist into NREM sleep stages, including the deep sleep stages, when delta brain waves are supposed to be predominant. As a result of this constant intrusion of wakefulness, sleep quality is greatly harmed, and because deep sleep is interspersed with the alpha rhythm throughout the night, the person gets up in the morning with aches, stiffness, and the sense of having been in a "twilight zone" all night.

Sleep and Immune Functions

Sleep loss may lower immune functions and thereby increase the vulnerability to certain physical ailments and prolong recovery periods. Every year, many of us suffer from viral infections. The influenza viral syndrome, or the flu, is commonly associated with complaints of fatigue, sleepiness, and a general malaise. Naturally, the most frequently prescribed cure, from a doctor or a grandmother, is to "get plenty of rest and sleep," but it is only recently that the relationship of sleep to immune functions has been examined closely. Researchers at the National Institute of Mental Health have found that sleep-deprived rats take longer to recover from infectious diseases than those allowed to sleep as much as they want to. These very preliminary results suggest that sleep may indeed aid in protecting us and in speeding our recuperation from some diseases. It is not yet clear whether the effects of sleep loss on immune functions are caused by the disease itself or from the stress that follows sleep deprivation. Indeed, sleep difficulties cause such mood disturbances as irritability, tension, and dysphoria, which may also affect recovery time.

Sleep Duration and Longevity

In a large survey of health and living habits sponsored by the American Cancer Society, people reporting either a very short (4 hours or less) or very long (more than 10 hours) sleep duration had a higher mortality rate than those with a sleep duration falling in the 7-to-8-hour range. The longest life expectancy was associated with a sleep duration of 7 to 7.9 hours. People using sleeping pills regularly had a mortality rate 1.5 times higher than those who never used sleeping pills. Although these figures suggest a link between sleep duration and longevity, we must be careful before drawing such a conclusion, because people who have excessively short or long sleep, or who use sleeping pills, often suffer from heart disease, diabetes, or other medical conditions that in themselves are associated with reduced longevity.

Sleep and Depression

Many psychological conditions are associated with sleep disturbances. Most of those are discussed in Chapter 3, but let's just say that almost anyone who has experienced a bout of depression is likely to have suffered concomitant sleep difficulty, most typically, early-morning awakening. In addition to this classic symptom, several other distinct changes in sleep patterns occur during an episode of major depression. We saw earlier that healthy young adults enter REM sleep only after spending 70 to 90 minutes in the different NREM stages and that the episodes of REM sleep increase in duration and intensity throughout the night. Drs. David Kupfer and Charles Reynolds, at the Western Psychiatric Institute and Clinics in Pittsburgh, have studied sleep in depressed patients for over two decades. They found that individuals with endogenous depression (not in reaction to a life crisis), compared with nondepressed people, get into REM sleep much more rapidly, often within 15 to 20 minutes, and spend more time in this state early on in the night. Their REM sleep is also more intense, and there is a corresponding decrease of the deep stages of sleep early in the night. These features of a shortened latency and increased amount of REM sleep may represent biological markers or traits of depression. In another line of research on sleep and depression, it has been found that sleep deprivation produces temporary mood improvements in a person with severe depression. This result, which is achieved with total or selective REM sleep deprivation, is in contrast with the more typical mood disturbances observed in people with milder but more chronic sleep disturbances.

These few examples illustrate how closely sleep is intertwined with mind and body matters. Although no one is completely immune from sleep difficulties, a healthy mind in a physically fit body enhances the chance of getting restful sleep; conversely, sound sleep may provide protection against physical and mental health problems.

THE EFFECTS OF SLEEP DEPRIVATION ON PERFORMANCE AND PUBLIC SAFETY

Sleep loss, whether self-induced or caused by an underlying disorder, can interfere with your job, social and family relationships, and can even place your life and that of others in jeopardy. The severity of these effects depends in part upon whether sleep loss is partial or total, and whether it is temporary or chronic in nature. Temporary sleep loss causes fatigue and decreases motivation, initiative, and creativity the next day. It may have limited effect on the performance of simple and repetitive motor tasks. For instance, you may find it difficult, after a sleepless night, to summon up the energy and imagination to design a new marketing plan for your company or write an article for a magazine; however, you may still be able to perform quite efficiently some other manual duties, such as typing memos at your computer terminal. Whereas the first task requires mental effort, the second can be performed in a more automated fashion.

With prolonged sleep deprivation, daytime sleepiness accumulates and all other deficits are aggravated. Attention span is reduced, concentration is impaired, and reaction time is prolonged. Judgments and problem-solving skills are also diminished. Perhaps the most serious consequence is daytime drowsiness, which often leads to microsleep episodes. These are very brief lapses, lasting only a few seconds, that intrude into wakefulness during routine daily activities, often unbeknown to the individual. If you are home watching television or reading the newspaper, the worst that can happen is that you will fall asleep. But falling asleep in a public place is likely to cause embarrassment and, at work, could jeopardize your job. Sleep loss and its consequences may also pose serious public health and safety hazards. The U.S. Department of Transportation estimates that up to 200,000 traffic accidents each year are related to sleepiness and that 20 percent of all drivers have dozed off at least once behind the wheel. More than half of night-shift workers acknowledge having fallen asleep on the job at least once. This human factor has been implicated in several major industrial accidents, all occurring in the middle of the night. Among the most publicized incidents are those at the Chernobyl nuclear plant in Ukraine, the gas explosion in Bhopal, India, and the *Exxon Valdez* oil transport grounding on the coast of Alaska.

Sleep deprivation, whether imposed voluntarily or caused by an underlying disorder, is likely to impair alertness and performance. It does not lead to a major change in personality, but, as we shall see in the next chapter, chronic insomnia may cause a great deal of personal distress and suffering, and diminish the quality of life.

In summary, we need to sleep at periodic intervals, and we need all the different kinds of sleep. Sleep serves dual functions—physical and psychological. NREM sleep is primarily involved in recuperating and restoring physical energy and perhaps in protecting the organism against diseases. REM sleep facilitates learning and memory consolidation, and may be involved in problem-solving and in adapting to our daily emotional experiences. The timing of our sleep is regulated by a biological clock, which itself is synchronized by the amount of daylight exposure and by environmental time markers. The effects of sleep deprivation are numerous, affecting daytime functioning, mood, quality of life, and public safety.

2
What Is Insomnia?

It's 1:00 A.M. and Donna has been struggling to fall asleep for the last two hours. From an important deadline coming up tomorrow, to what she might wear for dinner next Saturday, the same film of anxious thoughts mixed with mundane events keeps unrolling through her mind. She's tried counting sheep, staying focused on her breathing, or just making her mind blank, but nothing seems to rid her of those intrusive thoughts and slow down her racing mind. If anything, she's becoming more anxious and restless, tossing and turning to find a comfortable position. She doesn't want to open her eyes, but she feels compelled to check the clock and see how much time is left before she has to get up to go to work. Finally, from pure exhaustion, she falls asleep and sleeps soundly until the next morning.

Jeff doesn't have any trouble falling asleep. He is so exhausted when he hits the sack, around 10:30, that he usually falls asleep in 5 or 10 minutes. His problem is that he doesn't stay asleep. He wakes up one, two, or three times a night, for no apparent reason, and has trouble getting back to sleep. He is very careful not to do anything that will keep him awake, but he can't resist peeking at the clock. Then he thinks about unfinished business at the office or what is on the agenda for tomorrow. Eventually, he falls asleep again, only to wake up an hour or so later. Although he didn't at first think of this as a problem, it is taking its toll. Jeff has come to expect that if he wakes up, he's in for anywhere from 15 minutes to an hour of wakefulness. He often gets angry with himself when he is wide awake in the middle of the night and everyone else in the house is sound asleep.

Unlike Donna and Jeff, Betsy can fall asleep easily and stay asleep for a solid stretch of 5 or 6 hours. Her main problem is that she wakes up too early in the morning, typically at 4:00 or 5:00—and that's it for the night. She goes to the bathroom and quickly returns to bed, hoping to catch another wink before sunrise. It rarely works. So she lies in bed awake and worries about everything—depressive thoughts about herself, problems with the children, her life in general, and even about her inability to achieve better control of her sleep. When the clock finally goes off, she has to drag herself out of bed.

THE MANY FACES OF INSOMNIA

These scenarios illustrate three common types of insomnia. There may be problems falling asleep at bedtime (Donna), known as sleep-onset insomnia, waking up in the middle of the night and having trouble going back to sleep (Jeff), or waking too early in the morning (Betsy), both examples of sleep-maintenance insomnia. Difficulties initiating and maintaining sleep are not mutually exclusive, and the same person may suffer from sleep-onset insomnia, sleep-maintenance insomnia, or mixed onset and maintenance difficulties. The nature of the problem may also shift over time. Although not all people fit precisely into one of these categories, a subjective complaint of insomnia generally reflects unsatisfactory duration or quality of sleep. At times, there may be no apparent problem in going to sleep or staying asleep, yet the sleep is perceived as light, unrefreshing, or nonrestorative. Staying in the "twilight zone" (half awake, half asleep) most of the night can be a very frustrating and exhausting experience; thoughts keep intruding into your mind, and your awareness of the immediate surroundings may last the entire night, preventing the natural progression to a deep slumber.

There is no single definition of insomnia. Experts agree, however, that taking more than 30 minutes to fall asleep at bedtime or spending more than 30 minutes awake in the middle of the night, with a corresponding sleep time of less than 6.5 hours a night, represents an insomnia problem. A sleep efficiency of 85 percent is a good marker to distinguish normal sleep from clinical insomnia. Sleep efficiency is the ratio of time asleep, divided by time spent in bed, multiplied by 100. For example, if you spend on average 8 hours a night in bed and sleep for only 6 of those hours, your sleep efficiency would be 75 percent ($^6/_8 = .75 \times 100 = 75$ percent). Although most good sleepers fall asleep in 10 to 15 minutes, taking 15 to 30 minutes is certainly nothing to worry about. Conversely, those who fall asleep within 5 minutes or less are probably sleep-deprived and would do well to get more doze. Because there are individual differences in sleep needs, reduced sleep duration alone is not necessarily indicative of insomnia. If you sleep 6 or 7 hours a night and feel rested and alert the next day, you do not suffer from insomnia. If, though, you usually have trouble falling asleep or staying asleep three or more nights a week, and you've had the problem for more than a few weeks, you probably do have insomnia. Clinical features commonly used to diagnose insomnia are outlined in Table 2.1.

Table 2.1. INSOMNIA DIAGNOSTIC CRITERIA

- Subjective complaint of insomnia.
- Sleep-onset latency or time awake after sleep onset greater than 30 minutes; and total sleep time less than 6.5 hours or sleep efficiency lower than 85 percent.
- Sleep difficulties present 3 or more nights a week.
- Duration of insomnia longer than 1 month.
- Psychological distress and/or trouble with daytime social, family, or occupational functioning caused by sleeplessness.

Insomnia is a fairly subjective experience and, not unlike chronic pain, may be difficult to describe and even more difficult to quantify. Sleep perception does not always correspond to actual sleep when measured by electroencephalographic (EEG) monitoring of brain-wave patterns. Studies comparing a person's estimates of various sleep parameters often show some discrepancies between subjective estimates and objective recordings of sleep. For example, in comparison to EEG criteria, insomniacs tend to overestimate the time it takes them to fall asleep and to underestimate their total amount of sleep.

We noted in the preceding chapter the different stages of NREM sleep, progressing from light to deep sleep over the course of each cycle. When awakened from a light sleep (stage 1), insomniacs will often report that they were awake, whereas good sleepers are more likely to report they were sleeping, or they may simply be uncertain of their state at that moment. It isn't that poor sleepers are exaggerating their problems; rather, it may be that the accuracy of time estimation is correlated to the pleasantness of a situation. For instance, during sensory-deprivation experiments, where a person is floating in a huge tank of salt water and is cut off from all visual or sensory stimulations, there is a tendency to think less time has elapsed than actually has, as this is seen as a pleasant, calming experience. Conversely, lying awake in bed at night can be an unpleasant experience, causing the person to overestimate the time it takes to fall asleep. The chances are that you're falling asleep a little faster than you think and getting more sleep than you think. Nonetheless, if you perceive your sleep to be inadequate, you have insomnia.

SITUATIONAL AND CHRONIC SLEEP DIFFICULTIES

The duration of a sleep problem is another important dimension to consider in assessing the need for treatment. Virtually everyone experiences an occasional bout of insomnia, usually brought on by emotional turmoil, physical ailments, or jet lag. This type of acute insomnia usually lasts only a few days and there is no reason to be alarmed by it. When life returns to normal, sleep does too. At times, however, sleep difficulties may persist for a few weeks (short-term insomnia), months, or even years (chronic insomnia). Transient insomnia is often associated with more enduring stressors, like family, occupational, or personal relationship problems. Again, most people are likely to return to a normal sleep pattern after their life conditions return to normal. For some people, however, insomnia may become chronic. Perhaps the initial precipitating events—family problems or occupational stress—

become persistent in nature. Or it may be that the insomnia has developed a life of its own even after removal of the stressor or adjustment to its more permanent nature. Regardless of the origin, when sleep difficulties persist for more than a few weeks, it is time to do something about them.

Sometimes insomnia follows an intermittent path. It may be that you generally sleep well at home but not when you travel. Many students have trouble sleeping during the school year and get a break during holidays. Some women experience brief but recurrent episodes of fitful sleep during or just prior to menstruation. The "Sunday night insomnia" is another form of situational but recurring sleeplessness, often caused by sleeping late on weekends, a common practice among both poor and good sleepers. Some sleep late strictly for the pleasure of not having to wake up to the sound of an alarm clock. Others may be paying back the sleep debt they accumulated during the week as a result of long working hours, and still others may be trying to compensate for sleepless nights. Whatever the reason, it is natural to try to catch up by sleeping a little later in the morning or by napping during the day. A few extra hours of sleep may be enough to revitalize your mind and body. The net result, though, is that you may not be sleepy by your usual bedtime on Sunday night. By Monday or Tuesday night, however, your biological clock is reset and sleep is back to normal. The Sunday night insomnia is nothing to worry about as long as you, your family, and co-workers can deal with any Monday morning "blahs." If you have young children or multiple other obligations on your days off from work, you probably cannot afford the luxury of those few extra hours of sleep on weekends and therefore may be more immune to Sunday night insomnia. Sleeping in late on weekends, a healthy practice in those who are good sleepers, is generally discouraged for those who are prone to insomnia. In addition, Sunday may be a particularly bad night for those whose insomnia is aggravated by the apprehension of returning to a stressful job on Monday morning. We will return to this in Chapter 6.

Who Has Insomnia and How Common Is It?

Virtually everyone is affected by sleep difficulties at one period or another in a lifetime. Surveys show that insomnia strikes more than a third of the population, men and women of all ages, at any given time. For example, a recent Gallup survey of almost 2000 adults found that 27 percent reported occasional insomnia. An additional 9 percent were plagued with chronic insomnia, struggling to sleep night after night for weeks, months, or even years. Insomnia complaints are twice as frequent in women as in men. It is unclear whether women are at greater risk for sleep problems or simply more inclined to report trouble sleeping. Since insomnia is perceived by some as a sign of weakness or diminished self-control, some men may suffer in silence. Interestingly, objective laboratory assessments show that the sleep patterns of men, particularly older men, tend to be more disrupted than those of women.

The incidence of sleep problems increases with age, and the nature of the complaint also changes. More than 20 percent of people aged 60 or older report serious trouble sleeping at night. As we grow older, sleep is lighter and less time is spent in the deeper stages. Consequently, frequent and prolonged awakening is particularly common and troublesome in seniors, whereas trouble falling asleep at bedtime, or pure lack of sleep, is more prevalent among younger people. Although age in itself produces changes in sleep patterns, and deteriorating health can also disrupt sleep, it is important for seniors to realize that insomnia is not an inevitable consequence of aging. Many older people experience sleep disturbances above and beyond what might be expected from the aging and health factors alone, and could benefit from some simple changes in sleep habits and schedules. I will discuss this further in Chapter 14.

Insomnia is by far the most common of all sleep disorders. Along with the common cold and pain, sleep complaints are among the most frequent health problems brought to the attention of physicians. An interesting but unfortunate paradox is that although half of insomnia sufferers consider their sleep problem serious enough to seek professional help, only a small minority actually seek or receive treatment. In the Gallup survey mentioned above, fewer than 5 percent of chronic insomniacs said they had previously talked to their doctors about insomnia, another 28 percent said they had discussed their sleep problems during visits for other purposes, and a full 67 percent had never discussed it with their physician. While many of those "silent sufferers" could benefit from some professional help, it seems that some have come to believe their insomnia is not a genuine clinical problem, that nothing can be done about it, or that a sleeping pill is the only treatment available. Frankly, the lack of training of most doctors and other health professionals in recognizing and treating insomnia may be responsible for this epidemic of silent suffering. Not knowing what to do besides prescribing a sleeping pill, a doctor may be quick to disregard an insomnia complaint or blame it on stress or aging. How often have you been told not to worry about it, that it will go away? Although there is some truth to that, it does not address the problem and can be very frustrating for the person who has to struggle with sleepless nights.

WHAT ARE THE RISK FACTORS?

There is no single personality profile that best characterizes all individuals who suffer insomnia. There are, however, a number of psychological characteristics or traits that seem to place some individuals at greater risk of insomnia. Hyperarousal is one of the most central features. It refers to a state of mental pressure, tension, or to a "racing mind" that just can't shut off at night. In our first clinical vignette, Donna exemplifies this feature. The accompanying physiological state is often one of muscular tension, faster brain-waves and heart rate, and higher body temperature. While some people thrive on such a high arousal level during the day, which can translate into more energy and increased productivity, the same people may have a hard time unwinding at bedtime; they remain "keyed up." An obsessional thinking style, a common characteristic of chronic worriers, is another characteristic that places some individuals at greater risk of experiencing sleep difficulties. People with this feature are often anxious or hypervigilant and just can't seem to let go at bedtime. The tendency

Table 2.2. COMMON INSOMNIA RISK FACTORS

- Cognitive and physical hyperarousal
- Obsessive thinking style
- Tendency to repress emotions
- Medical and psychological problems
- Female gender
- Increasing age
- Family history of insomnia

to repress one's emotions may translate into more somatic problems, including insomnia. Although everyone has daily hassles, people who do not speak their mind during the day have a tendency to take their problems to bed at night and worry about them; and attempting to get rid of these intrusive thoughts just doesn't seem to work. If some of those traits are characteristic of your personality, you may be at greater risk of insomnia.

As sleep is very sensitive to both psychological problems and physical ailments, individuals with either of these complaints are more predisposed to disrupted sleep than those who are psychologically and physically healthy. Combined with increased medical problems and medication use in late life, aging of the brain places older people at greater risk for most sleep disorders. In general, women seem to be at greater risk for insomnia, whereas men tend to suffer more frequently from sleep-related interrupted breathing, or a disorder such as sleep apnea. The reason for the higher predisposition of women is not entirely clear, but hormonal changes during menopause may enhance the risk. A family history of insomnia is also a risk factor, though it is unclear whether it is the result of a genetic contribution or maladaptive sleep habits picked up from parents. Narcolepsy, a sleep disorder characterized by sudden and unpredictable sleep attacks, has a definite genetic component. No such hereditary component has been identified among insomnia sufferers. It is important to realize that these risk factors do not mean that you will develop insomnia. Even if you recognize in yourself some of those features, sleep patterns can be changed without a complete change in your personality style.

THE IMPACT OF CHRONIC INSOMNIA

Loss of proper sleep at night is likely to have adverse effects the next day on job performance, psychological well-being, quality of life, and even physical health. In the preceding chapter, we reviewed some of the effects of sleep loss observed in controlled sleep-deprivation experiments. Now we will examine the effects of chronic insomnia, which are often more subtle and more difficult to measure objectively. Nevertheless, they are just as important, because it is often those feared consequences or perceived adverse effects, rather than actual lack of sleep, that prompt insomnia sufferers to seek professional help.

Sandy, a 42-year-old data analyst, had suffered from chronic insomnia since her college years. In her testimony before the National Commission of Sleep Disorders Research on Capitol Hill in Washington, D.C., she eloquently described the effects of her prolonged battle with insomnia:

The effects of my sleepless nights have been quite detrimental to my job performance, emotional stability, and physical well-being. Over the years I have lost the initiative to take on new challenges, and even simple day-to-day tasks seem overwhelming. Often I am so groggy during the day that it is difficult to concentrate for long periods of time on complex tasks. I have found it difficult to motivate myself to undertake new projects or complete projects already under way. I dread going to work every day, because it is a constant battle just to stay awake at my desk. The emotional effects from insomnia and the chronic fatigue have been very debilitating to my personal and professional life. When I get home from work I have no energy to keep up with friendships and no interest to develop new ones. I have frequently experienced an overwhelming sense of despair and helplessness. Over the past five years, I have suffered from chronic sinus and bronchial infections, which have caused me to take 8 to 10 days of sick leave every year. I feel that sleep loss and chronic fatigue have made me more susceptible to these infections.

This testimony illustrates quite clearly the debilitating effects of chronic sleep difficulties on Sandy's personal and professional life.

Let's examine in more detail the problems commonly associated with sleepless nights.

Daytime Fatigue and Performance

Daytime fatigue is extremely common among those who suffer from chronic insomnia. This often translates into mental lethargy and difficulty with concentration and memory, which in turn slow down information processing. Motivation is also diminished, and great effort is needed to accomplish what is usually a simple and routine task. Physical clumsiness may also make you more prone to accidents after a sleepless night. Moments of inattention can cause you to misplace things or to question whether you have already done something you had planned to do. In the worst scenario, lapses in attention while driving can be fatal, to you or someone else on the road.

Surprisingly, the feeling of sleepiness during the day is not one of the characteristics of severe insomniacs. Insomnia sufferers are usually keyed up during the day as well as at night. In the Multiple Sleep Latency Test, sleep-disorder patients are offered five 20-minute naps at 2-hour intervals throughout the day. The speed with which they fall asleep provides an objective measure of sleepiness. Whereas those who suffer from narcolepsy and sleep apnea fall asleep within 5 minutes, which is considered a dangerous level of sleepiness, insomniacs may take 12 to 15 minutes or may not fall asleep at all. Thus, despite clear signs of fatigue and mental tiredness, there is little evidence of physiological sleepiness.

Psychological Well-Being

Acute insomnia can cause considerable emotional distress, especially if you perceive it as an indication of loss of control. Sometimes patients who have recently had a sleepless episode show up at our clinic in a state of panic. They fear they may never be able to get to sleep again. There is a great deal of anxiety about what may happen to their mind and body if they can't regain control of what was once taken for granted. Not everyone worries about disturbed sleep to that extent, especially when the sleep problem is situational in nature. But those who have to struggle nightly with a sleep problem often become more irritable, tense, and depressed. People with chronic sleep disturbances may also develop a sense of learned helplessness. No matter what they do, nothing seems to help or to make sleep any more predictable. It is no surprise, then, that a person is at greater risk of developing depression when insomnia persists for more than a year and is left untreated.

Insomnia can also take its toll on one's ability to enjoy family and social relationships. It is more difficult to cope with minor irritations after a poor night's sleep; interactions with friends, family members, or co-workers are less enjoyable. At times, there is even a sense of social alienation, since one can easily feel intimidated or irritated by others, which leads to social withdrawal and avoidance of people.

Physical Health

The effects of insomnia on physical health are not as clear as those on psychological well-being, although those who suffer from insomnia express a great deal of concern and fear about the negative impact of sleep problems on their health. As was clearly illustrated in Sandy's testimony, some people feel that their immune system is run down and that they are more susceptible to a cold, the flu, or infection because of chronic insomnia. These effects have been documented in animal studies, but there is currently no clear cause-and-effect relationship suggesting that insomnia in humans has any lasting ill effects on physical health, although there is no question that waking from a poor night's sleep is rude and hard on one's body. At times, your body aches all over. But whether that is the result of sleep loss or the psychological distress that often accompanies sleeplessness remains unclear. Again, it is important to remember that, although sleep efficiency and quality may be impaired, the actual amount of sleep loss is usually modest in most insomniacs.

The Economic Costs

The National Commission of Sleep Disorders Research estimated that American people pay about $392 million for prescription drugs to induce sleep and another $84 million for over-the-counter sleep aids. The annual expenses associated with visits to physicians and mental-health professionals for insomnia is estimated at about $500 million. People with insomnia are generally more preoccupied with their health and tend to use health-related services more frequently than good sleepers, further taxing the health care system. The indirect costs of sick days, diminished performance on the job, and even industrial or motor vehicle accidents resulting from sleep disturbances are enormous. All these direct and indirect costs, combined with the human suffering and diminished quality of life associated with insomnia, are astronomical.

Do You Suffer from Insomnia?

Now that you have learned about the nature, types, and impact of insomnia, let's examine whether you have an insomnia problem and, if so, what kind it is, and whether you should pursue this self-management program. Take a few minutes to answer the insomnia quiz in Table 2.3 and compare your responses with the diagnostic criteria outlined in Table 2.1. If you meet most of those five criteria, you should try this sleep-training program. Even if you do not meet all the criteria, you may still benefit from the program and perhaps prevent the development of more severe and more chronic sleep difficulties. You will note some questions about the use of sleep aids in the insomnia quiz; we will address this issue in more detail in Chapter 11. For now, however, if you are using prescribed or over-the-counter sleeping pills or alcohol as a sleep aid, this may be masking your sleep problem. Those substances are recommended only for short-term use; so if you have been using a sleep aid for more than a few weeks, it is time to do something about that too; you may also benefit from the strategies recommended in this book.

If you answered yes to any of the questions in the last section, possible causes of insomnia, make sure to read Chapters 3 and 12, which describe several conditions that may contribute to your insomnia and require medical attention before you begin this program.

Table 2.3. INSOMNIA QUIZ

What Kind of Sleep Problems Do You Have?

Do you have trouble falling asleep?

Do you wake up in the middle of the night and have trouble going back to sleep?

Do you wake up too early in the morning and can't get back to sleep?

Do you get up in the morning feeling as if you have been in a light sleep all night?

Situational or Chronic Insomnia

How many nights per week do you have difficulty sleeping? Does the difficulty occur on particular nights?

How long have you had trouble sleeping?

How Does Insomnia Affect You During the Day?

Is your daytime energy reduced by poor sleep at night (are you fatigued, tired, exhausted)?

Is it difficult to function during the day as a result of poor sleep (do you have concentration and memory problems)?

Is your mood affected by insomnia (are you irritable, tensed, depressed, confused)?

Are you concerned about sleeplessness or about the way it affects you during the day?

Use of Sleep Aids

How often do you use a prescribed sleeping pill?

How often do you use an over-the-counter sleep aid?

How often do you use alcohol as a sleep aid?

Possible Causes of Insomnia

Do you suffer from a medical or emotional disorder?

Has your sleep partner noticed that you snore or that you stop breathing while you sleep?

Are your legs restless at bedtime?

Has your sleep partner noticed that you jerk or kick your legs while sleeping?

3

The Various Causes
of Insomnia

Sleep experts have identified a host of factors that can produce insomnia—psychological, medical, pharmacological, environmental, and many more. Perhaps the two most important are psychological and medical. As sleep is very sensitive to changes in emotional or physical status, it is often the first casualty during a period of emotional crisis or ill health. Insomnia can be induced by the excessive use of caffeine, nicotine, alcohol, or even sleeping pills. Some prescribed medications or over-the-counter preparations can disrupt sleep as well. A number of concealed sleep disorders may be at the origin of an insomnia problem. Jet lag and shift work can place our biological clock out of synch with the outside world, producing sleepiness when everyone is awake and insomnia when everyone is sleeping. Because insomnia can be a symptom of so many different conditions, a detailed evaluation is usually necessary to determine the most likely contributing factors, keeping in mind that the problem is rarely caused by a single factor. Often, it is the result of several factors. Let's turn to each of them now.

Stress, anxiety, and depression are without a doubt the most common causes of insomnia. Virtually everyone faces, at least periodically, minor stressors, irritations, or hassles—at home, at work, or while commuting in between. They may involve conflicts with an employer or a co-worker, relationship problems or disagreements with a significant other or relatives, or even the aggravation of a constant traffic jam. People react differently. Some are equipped with effective strategies to cope with daytime stressors, while others can put aside everything at bedtime and sleep "like a log," no matter what took place during the day. Perhaps more sensitive to these same daytime irritations, others remain keyed up and inevitably experience sleep difficulties.

Regardless of the psychological make-up of a person, there are some major life events that interfere with sleep, at least temporarily. The break-up of a relationship, the death of a loved one, the loss of a job, or impending surgery will almost always trigger sleep disturbances, even in the best sleepers in the world. Under such circumstances, insomnia is a natural response, often part of a depressive episode, a grieving process, or anxiety regarding a life-threatening condition. Sleep will usually, but not always, return to normal once the stressor has disappeared or the person has adjusted to its more permanent nature.

Sleep difficulties may also be associated with a more deeply rooted psychological disorder. For instance, insomnia is a symptom of several anxiety and depressive conditions. Trouble falling asleep is especially common in those who suffer from anxiety disorders; early-morning awakening is a classic complaint in people who are depressed. The nature of the sleep difficulty can vary from one person to another and may even fluctuate over time with the underlying disorders. I will briefly review here some of the main symptoms of anxiety and depression.

In *generalized anxiety disorders,* people worry excessively and chronically, not only about sleep, but about such life circumstances as health, family, job, finances. Although there may be reasons to justify their behavior, people who suffer from this condition tend always to anticipate the worst. The worrying is uncontrollable. Generalized anxiety is also characterized by symptoms like restlessness, being easily fatigued, having difficulty in concentrating, muscle tension, and, in most cases, trouble sleeping. In *obsessive-compulsive disorders* (OCD), people are consumed by obsessive thinking and ritualistic or repetitive behaviors. For example, convinced that his or her body is in danger of contamination with any outside contact, a person with an OCD may spend several hours daily washing and cleaning. Although people who suffer from OCD recognize that their fears are not justified, the ritualistic behavior serves to reduce their underlying anxiety.

Panic attacks are circumscribed episodes of excessive fears and anxiety that occur spontaneously in the absence of actually threatening conditions. A person may suddenly, for no apparent reason, fear that he or she will die, faint, or simply lose control. When such fear arises in a public place, it is generally accompanied by an escape from that situation and, eventually, by total avoidance of similar situations. Typically occurring in the daytime, panic attacks can also arise at night with perhaps even greater intensity. True panic attacks, however, are usually distinguished from nocturnal panic or anxiety attacks resulting from sleeplessness and the fear of not being able to function the next day.

Individuals who suffer from *post-traumatic stress disorders,* caused by a major psychological trauma, often experience flashbacks of the traumatic events, accompanied by intense levels of psychological distress, apprehension, and various sleep difficulties, including insomnia, nightmares, or sleep terrors. These symptoms are particularly common among war veterans, victims of sexual abuse or rape, and among those exposed to natural disasters. Surveys of the San Francisco Bay area residents following the 1989 earthquake revealed an increased incidence of nightmares and distressing dreams. Likewise, high rates of sleep problems and nightmares, along with increased fear, apprehension, and stress, were observed among Israeli residents during and after the 1991 Gulf War. One may expect similar findings among victims' relatives and residents of Oklahoma City following the bombing of the federal building in April 1995.

Insomnia is also frequently a sign of an underlying *depression;* subtypes of depression vary in intensity, duration, and fluctuation over time. Typical depressive symptoms include sadness, lack of interest in people, inability to enjoy activities that used to be pleasurable, fatigue and diminished energy, low self-esteem and feelings of worthlessness, suicidal thoughts, poor appetite, and sleep disturbances. Episodes of major depression usually last a few weeks to a few months. Sometimes the depressive symptoms are less intense but more chronic in nature, a condition called dysthymia. In either case, sleep difficulties are almost always present. These may involve trouble falling asleep, staying asleep, or both. Most typically a person who suffers from major depression wakes prematurely in the morning and can't return to sleep. Insomnia can also be part of *manic-depressive illness,* in which episodes of severe depression alternate with periods of excessively high energy, activity levels, grandiose ideas, and the decreased need for sleep. In this case, a person may oversleep during a depressive episode and go with little sleep during the manic episode.

If you think that you suffer from one of these anxiety or depressive conditions, you should seek professional help. Sleep will usually, but not always, improve as the anxiety or mood disorder is treated with psychotherapy, medication, or both. When the anxiety or depression are severe enough, treatment should be directed at the underlying condition. It is quite possible, however, that you may experience some of those symptoms but without the intensity described above. For those who suffer and those who treat sleep disorders, a dilemma that often arises is determining which of the psychological or sleep problems came first—the classic chicken-or-egg puzzle. There is a strong relationship between sleep and emotional disturbances, but the extent to which is the cause and which the consequence is not always clear. What seems apparent, however, is that chronically disturbed sleep causes psychological distress in some individuals, and insomnia may aggravate the difficulties of those already afflicted with emotional problems. The bottom line is that you should talk to a psychologist, a psychiatrist, or your family doctor if you experience persistent psychological and sleep difficulties that interfere with your job, family, and with the quality of your life. You don't have to suffer.

THE MEDICAL CAUSES

Acute and chronic medical illnesses can disrupt sleep because of underlying symptoms (pain), the medical or surgical procedures used to alleviate those symptoms, or emotional distress about the illness.

Congestive heart failure and chronic-obstructive pulmonary disease almost inevitably disrupt sleep patterns because of diminished blood supply, impaired respiration, and decreased oxygen. The underlying anxiety and fear of dying that may accompany cardiovascular and respiratory problems will often worsen the sleep disturbances. An endocrine condition such as hyperthyroidism—an overproductive thyroid gland—can cause insomnia, and appropriate therapy will usually alleviate the difficulty. Gastrointestinal diseases, such as reflux, hiatal hernia, or peptic ulcer, can produce difficulty in falling asleep or cause nocturnal awakenings as a result of acid regurgitation or heartburn. Changing diet, raising the head of one's bed, and using an antacid medication may reduce these symptoms. Renal diseases and diabetes can also cause sleep difficulties because of diminished blood circulation in the extremities. Two common problems among diabetic patients and patients on dialysis are the restless legs syndrome and periodic limb movements. These sleep disorders, which are described in Chapter 12, can give rise to insomnia, daytime sleepiness, or a combination of both.

Since the main switchboard controlling sleep and wakefulness is located in the brain, any neurological disease or brain injury will interfere with a normal sleep-wake cycle. Depending on the severity and the specific site of brain involvement, neurological diseases or injury may produce insomnia at night and excessive sleepiness during the day. Patients with Alzheimer's disease, a degenerative disease of the brain, have very disrupted sleep patterns, characterized by short periods of sleep intruding on almost every hour of the day, and extended periods of wakefulness interfering with nighttime sleep. The problem is compounded by confusion and nocturnal wandering, which put a significant burden on caregivers and often lead to institutionalization.

Almost any condition producing pain or physical discomfort is likely to disrupt sleep. More than half of those who suffer from such chronic conditions as arthritis, osteoporosis, fibrositis, or low back pain report that pain interferes with their sleep. For many of those people, chronic pain means chronic sleep disturbances. In turn, a person who does not get a good night's sleep will often find his or her pain more intense and unpleasant during the day; not surprisingly, disturbed sleep is for many people the most disabling consequence of chronic pain. If sleep is adequate at night, they may at least cope more effectively with their pain during the day.

For some women with premenstrual symptoms (PMS), the quality and amount of sleep may fluctuate with the menstrual cycle. Sleep is of poorer quality and of shorter duration in the few days preceding the onset of the menses; it usually improves shortly afterward and remains essentially normal through the rest of the menstrual cycle. Some women may experience hypersomnia rather than insomnia; they feel excessively sleepy during the day. Women with PMS symptoms like irritability, depression, and/or anxious moods are particularly prone to develop one of these periodic sleep disturbances.

Menopause also can affect sleep. Hormonal changes occurring during this life cycle are frequent precipitating factors of sleep disturbances. "Hot flashes" are the most frequent cause of nocturnal awakenings in menopausal women; the sensation of increased body temperature causes the person to wake up in "night sweats." Estrogen therapy is helpful in correcting the underlying problem. Sometimes, however, a person who has always been a good sleeper may become very nervous about sleep pattern changes, and that anxiety may be enough to set the stage for more chronic sleep disturbances. It is not uncommon in our sleep clinic for women to report their first insomnia episode during menopause. Even when other menopausal symptoms have been resolved or appropriately controlled with hormonal supplement therapy, they continued to suffer sleep disturbances.

Allergies and any infection affecting breathing may disrupt sleep in otherwise good sleepers or worsen insomnia in those who already suffer from it. Sleep difficulties of this nature are especially prevalent when the pollen is released in the spring. The sinus and breathing problems caused by allergies are usually temporary and are best treated with antihistamines.

PRESCRIBED AND RECREATIONAL DRUGS AND ALCOHOL

It is not unusual for a prescribed medication that is effective in treating a particular problem to produce another as a side effect. Several drugs prescribed for medical or psychiatric illnesses can cause insomnia, especially when taken at bedtime. Some beta blockers prescribed for hypertension may do the same. For example, propranolol (Inderal) and clonidine are often associated with insomnia and nightmares. Diuretics may also interfere with sleep by causing frequent nocturnal urination. Some bronchodilators used in the treatment of asthma (e.g., theodur) have stimulating effects and interfere with sleep onset when taken at bedtime. Most steroid drugs (e.g., prednisone) prescribed for pain-related conditions can impair sleep. Thyroid preparations may cause insomnia, especially if the dosage is not exactly right; too large a dose for a hypothyroid condition can bring about hyperthyroidism and insomnia.

Some antidepressant medications have sedative properties, so they are sometimes prescribed in small dosages for the treatment of insomnia. Other antidepressant drugs, however, have a more energizing effect and may well interfere with sleep when used at bedtime. Among those are such popular drugs as fluoxetine (Prozac) and older antidepressant medications like imipramine (Tofranil) and protriptyline (Vivactil). Benzodiazepines are the medications most commonly used to control daytime anxiety and to induce sleep at night. Although sleeping pills may be helpful when used on a short-term basis, prolonged and nightly utilization of hypnotic medications may become part of the sleep problem. Drug-induced sleep is clearly not of the same quality as natural sleep. Most sleeping pills lengthen the total duration of sleep but decrease or eliminate the amount of deep sleep a person gets. Also, the chronic use of sleeping pills usually leads to tolerance and habituation. This type of drug-dependent insomnia is also known as iatrogenic insomnia, a disease that is caused by its treatment. Withdrawal from sleeping pills or from anti-anxiety drugs can cause significant rebound insomnia. Under withdrawal conditions, sleep may be worse than it was before, sometimes prompting a return to the medicine cabinet. We will return to this condition and learn how to solve it in Chapter 11.

A variety of over-the-counter medications can produce insomnia. Most appetite-suppressant preparations, for example, contain a stimulant that is naturally incompatible with sleep. And, while cold remedies contain an antihistamine, which produces drowsiness in most people, some people have a paradoxical reaction and become restless, fidgety, and sleepless.

Although many medications can cause insomnia as a side effect, not everyone using them will necessarily experience it. It is good practice to discuss potential side effects of any medication with your doctor and pharmacist. It may be possible for you to switch to a different drug or to change the schedule of administration in order to minimize the interference with your sleep.

Recreational drugs such as caffeine and nicotine are central nervous system stimulants and disrupt sleep even in those who claim it has no effect on their sleep. Laboratory recordings of the sleep patterns in persons using caffeine close to bedtime show that it takes them longer to fall asleep and that their sleep is lighter and more fitful. Similar findings are obtained for heavy smokers. Unlike caffeine and nicotine, alcohol is a central nervous system depressant. One might expect, then, that it would improve sleep. A nightcap at bedtime may indeed facilitate sleep onset in a tense person; it also produces deeper sleep in the early part of the night. A major inconvenience, however, is that sleep becomes more fitful and interrupted as the alcohol is metabolized during the second part of the night. There may also be an excessive amount of REM sleep at that time. Premature awakening in the morning without being able to return to sleep is also frequent. Along with its ill effects on health in general, alcohol abuse greatly impairs sleep patterns. The drinking person is usually unaware of sleep problems during a binge episode, but becomes acutely aware of his or her inability to sleep and of the severe nightmares endured during the withdrawal period. Residual sleep impairment often lasts for weeks or even months after the person returns to sobriety. Unfortunately, this may become so incapacitating and distressing that the person will relapse into drinking as a way to get some sleep. The price to pay, however, is that during the next withdrawal sleep will be just as disturbed as it was before the relapse.

ENVIRONMENTAL CONDITIONS

Various environmental conditions can result in insomnia: noise, light, excessive temperature, an uncomfortable mattress, or movements of a bed partner. Almost everyone has been kept awake at night by noisy traffic, loud music, or a neighbor's barking dog. A snoring or restless bed partner is another common source of sleep disruption; at times, it may precipitate a move to different sleeping quarters.

An interesting study conducted by the British psychologist Dr. Jim Horne found that couples sharing the same bed undergo more sleep disruptions than those sleeping alone. About half of the time a partner moves, he or she triggers a movement by the other partner within the next 30 seconds. While most participants subjectively thought they slept better with their partners beside them, because they felt more secure, most participants actually slept longer and with fewer interruptions when they slept alone. A member of a younger couple is more disturbed by the mate's movements than an older couple. Couples who have shared the same bed for years get accustomed to each other's movements. Newlyweds, on the other hand, may need some time to get accustomed to sharing a bed and adjusting to the other's movements and, possibly, snoring. Sleeping in a king-size bed can make a world of difference.

Unless you have proper drapes or blinds, daylight can be troublesome for the shift worker trying to sleep during the day. A room temperature that is too hot or too cold will also interfere with anyone's proper rest. Insomnia in hospitalized patients is perhaps the most common example of environmentally induced insomnia. Excessive noise, lighting, and the need for medical procedures can disrupt sleep even in those who usually have no insomnia problems. Older adults have lighter sleep and may be most susceptible to environmental causes of insomnia.

OTHER SLEEP AND CIRCADIAN DISORDERS

Sometimes insomnia is the presenting symptom, but the underlying problem has to do with another sleep or circadian disorder—sleep apnea, restless legs syndrome or periodic limb movements, jet lag, shift work, parasomnias. Those disorders and their most prominent symptoms are reviewed in Chapters 10 and 12.

HOW SITUATIONAL SLEEP DIFFICULTIES EVOLVE INTO CHRONIC INSOMNIA

So far we have seen that there are many sources of sleep disruptions—psychiatric, medical, drug-related, environmental, and so on. Some people may be at greater risk, but, under highly stressful conditions, virtually everyone will suffer from sleep disturbances. Fortunately, the insomnia usually is situational and time-limited. Sleep returns to normal after the precipitating factor has been removed or the person has accommodated to its more permanent nature. For a substantial number of people, though, sleep difficulties will continue even after the initial precipitant is no longer present. Then insomnia develops a life of its own and becomes independent of what triggered it in the first place. It is here that psychological factors play a major role in contributing to the development of chronic insomnia.

By psychological factors I am referring specifically to behaviors (sleep habits) and cognitions (beliefs and attitudes about sleep). During the initial phase of sleep difficulty, people who are prone to insomnia may develop conditioned reactions that are incompatible with sleep. For example, after several nights of poor sleep, a person may come to associate certain temporal (bedtime routines) and contextual (bedroom surroundings) stimuli or cues with apprehension, worry, and the fear of being unable to fall asleep. While there was a time in the past that activities such as putting on pajamas, brushing teeth, and getting into bed were associated with drowsiness, these same rituals have now become associated with sleeplessness. With repeated occurrences, the negative associations lead to increased muscle tension, worries, and to difficulty falling or staying asleep. In reaction to this sleeplessness, a person may become excessively worried about his or her inability to sleep (''Am I losing control?) and about the consequences (''How will I be able to function?). Further compounding the problem, some will engage in maladaptive sleep habits (e.g., excessive time spent in bed, irregular sleep-wake schedules, and daytime napping), which, although

Figure 3.1. The Vicious Cycle of Performance Anxiety and Sleeplessness

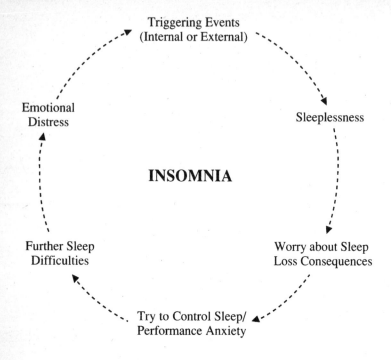

helpful in the short term, become part of the problem in the long run. The result of this chain reaction is a vicious cycle of insomnia, fear of sleeplessness, further sleep disturbances, and more emotional distress.

THE VICIOUS CYCLE OF PERFORMANCE ANXIETY AND SLEEPLESSNESS

Performance anxiety is one of the most important culprits in causing insomnia to persist over time. This type of anxiety arises when the desire to control or excel at something backfires and impairs performance. For instance, when you attempt to control sleep, perhaps because you're afraid of the consequences of insomnia the next day, you add to the pressure in yourself and thereby prolong wakefulness. Trying to sleep, then, is the worst mistake you can make. You simply cannot force yourself to sleep as you may be able to force wakefulness.

This type of performance anxiety is also found among couples with sex problems. Men can't produce an erection on demand, and women can't become orgasmic on command. Excessive attempts at controlling arousal and orgasm backfire, resulting in sexual dysfunctions that are caused strictly by performance anxiety. The only thing you can really do to facilitate orgasm in this situation is to change your thinking and various behaviors. Likewise, to short-circuit the vicious cycle of insomnia, you will need to alter thinking (beliefs and attitudes) and behavioral patterns (habits).

As we have seen in this chapter, insomnia can be a symptom of a multitude of underlying disorders, or it may be a disorder in itself. What complicates matters is that the various causes of insomnia are not mutually exclusive. In fact, very few people have insomnia that can be attributed to a single cause. For this reason, a comprehensive and careful evaluation is essential to sorting things out and making an accurate diagnosis. In the next chapter, we shall discuss what you can expect should you sign up for an evaluation at a sleep disorders clinic.

4

Should You Go to a Sleep Clinic?

The self-management program described in the next several chapters is intended primarily for those who suffer from common insomnia. As we saw, insomnia is often complicated by a number of medical and psychological disorders that may require professional attention before you undertake this program. In addition, there are many other sleep disorders that can be diagnosed and treated only by sleep specialists. In this chapter we'll review some symptoms that should be brought to the attention of sleep professionals, as well as indications that an overnight sleep study may be useful. We'll also review what you can expect when you sign up for a sleep clinic, how sleep is measured, the cost of an overnight sleep study, the answers to some commonly asked questions.

What to Expect from a Sleep Disorders Clinic

The specific procedures of each sleep clinic may vary but will generally involve some of the following steps. After you have been referred by your family doctor or have made an appointment yourself, you will be sent questionnaires and symptom checklists, along with a sleep log to keep for a week or two before the scheduled appointment. During your initial office visit, your sleep doctor (a physician, psychologist, or both) will review this information with you and will obtain a detailed sleep history and review with you symptoms of various sleep disorders. A medical history and a physical examination will provide detailed personal information. Laboratory blood tests may also be ordered. If the suspected problem is insomnia, a psychological evaluation may also be conducted to determine whether anxiety, depression, or other psychological factors are contributing to the sleep problem. This will help in establishing a preliminary diagnosis and determine whether an overnight sleep evaluation is needed.

Sleep clinics have several private bedrooms available for overnight evaluations. Special care is taken that these bedrooms are as quiet as possible and resemble hotel rooms rather than hospital rooms. It is important for the environment to be as much like home as possible, so most rooms have a television set, a radio, and a private bathroom. In our clinic, we also encourage the patient to bring his or her own pillow, since this is such a personal belonging. Other than that, all you need to bring are pajamas, some reading if you care for it, and any medications you may be using at home for hypertension, arthritis, or other illness. If you have been using sleep medications, talk to your doctor about the specific procedures to follow regarding their continued use or disuse. Some will prefer you taper off your medications one or two weeks before the test so that your sleep patterns can be monitored under drug-free conditions. If, however, you feel dependent on your sleeping pills, and are afraid of not sleeping at all during the test, you may not wish to discontinue them immediately. In our clinic, we usually conduct the test while the patient continues using medications as usual, and only after the sleep test do we design a specific treatment plan to taper off the medication over a period of several weeks.

On the night of the evaluation, you will be asked to arrive at the clinic several hours before your usual bedtime. The staff technician will need about an hour to prepare you and other patients for the sleep test. Once the hook-up procedures are completed, you will be allowed some time to relax, read, or watch television. Again, the specifics of each clinic vary, but overnight sleep evaluations are usually considered an outpatient procedure, and medication, food, and toilet articles are not provided. So be sure to check with your sleep clinic coordinator before you set out for your overnight test. After calibrating the apparatus and turning the lights out, the technician will monitor your sleep from an adjacent control room. There is a two-way intercom system allowing communication between yourself and the technician, and a closed-circuit video system is also in place to record any unusual behaviors during sleep.

How Is Sleep Measured?

Sleep is measured by three types of electrical signals: the electroencephalogram (EEG) records brain-wave activity, the electro-oculogram (EOG) measures eye movements, and the electromyogram (EMG) registers muscle tension (see Figure 4.1). Small electrodes (sensors) glued to the scalp (EEG) or taped to the skin (EMG, EOG) record these signals. The sensors are linked to a small control box that is plugged into the wall behind your bed, and the signals are amplified and simultaneously transmitted to a recording machine (polygraph) or to a computer screen located in the control room. These three channels (about 7 to 8 electrodes) are sufficient to indicate all your sleep stages through the night. Several additional sensors may also be used to monitor your respiration, heart rate, and leg movements, especially when sleep disorders other than insomnia are suspected, such as sleep apnea or periodic limb movements.

While this may sound complicated, it is not. Except for possible minor irritations of the skin from the application and removal of the sensors, sleep monitoring is a painless procedure. The signals are sent from your brain and body to the polygraph, not the reverse, so you don't need to worry about electric shocks being administered inadvertently. Still, you may wonder how in the world you will be able to sleep with all those wires and under such strange conditions. Although nothing is like sleeping at home, in your own bed and without monitoring devices, you can still move around quite freely. If you need to go to the bathroom during the sleep study, you can call the technician via the intercom, and the test will be easily interrupted for a moment. Naturally, it may take longer to fall asleep because you are in a strange environment, but, surprisingly, some insomniacs actually fall asleep more quickly because the cues that keep them awake at home are not present in the sleep laboratory. Others, who tend to be anxious at night

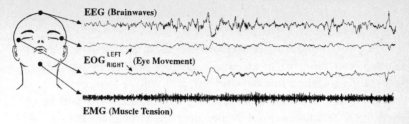

Figure 4.1. Sleep is measured by three types of physiological signals: the EEG records brain-wave patterns, the EOG measures eye movements, and the EMG registers muscle tension.

or live in undesirable neighborhoods, may simply feel more secure; knowing that it is a safe place, they can let go more easily. Patients suspected of sleep apnea or narcolepsy, for whom the main problem is staying awake, may actually doze off while being hooked up for the night.

A sleep test, called a polysomnogram, lasts between 6 and 8 hours. Although this is not always quite possible, most labs try to replicate as much as possible your usual bedtime and rising time, as well as your typical night's sleep duration. The technician wakes you up at your usual rising time. It takes just a few minutes to remove the electrodes, and you can take a shower and soon be ready to go home or directly to work. As the nighttime staff members leave to go get some sleep, other technicians come in to score your sleep record.

A one-night 8-hour study will generate about 1000 pages, or 1200 to 1500 feet of paper. Each page of paper represents 30 seconds of monitoring. With modernized technology, it is also possible to do a paperless study and record all the information on computers. Some laboratories are equipped to do home studies, where the information is either recorded on a tape or transmitted directly to the lab via telephone lines. The daytime technician scores all the data, page by page, according to standard criteria. Once this task is completed, a computer report documents how much time was spent in the different stages of sleep as well as any abnormalities in respiration and leg movements. The test results are analyzed by a sleep specialist, who then reviews it with you or your family doctor, and makes appropriate treatment recommendations.

If your main problem is in staying awake during the day (hypersomnia), you may also be asked to undergo a Multiple Sleep Latency Test (MSLT). During this daytime test, you will be told to wear your street clothes and refrain from drinking any caffeine. You will be offered five 20-minute naps at 2-hour intervals throughout the day. As they are during the nighttime test, your brain waves will be monitored to determine whether you fall asleep and, if you do, the type of sleep you get. The speed with which someone falls asleep provides an objective measure of daytime sleepiness. Falling asleep in 15 minutes or more is considered normal; within 5 and 10 minutes is the gray zone. Falling asleep in less than 5 minutes reflects a dangerous level of sleepiness, placing you at great risk for falling asleep in public situations. This level of alertness impairment is usually observed among those who suffer from narcolepsy, severe sleep apnea, or periodic limb movements. Insomniacs usually do not fall asleep on this test or, if they do, it may take more than 15 minutes. The MSLT is also a diagnostic test for narcolepsy. Hypersomniacs who are drug-free and who maintain a regular sleep schedule do not get into REM sleep during the day, except perhaps during a morning nap. Conversely, narcoleptic patients may enter REM sleep on several of the daytime naps.

When Should You Have a Sleep Test?

By definition, sleep precludes awareness of many abnormalities that might occur during this altered state of consciousness. Polysomnography is therefore essential for diagnosing and documenting several concealed sleep disorders and their severity. We'll briefly review here some of the most common symptoms that may suggest an underlying sleep disorder (see Chapter 12 for more information on these disorders) for which you should undergo an overnight sleep evaluation.

If your main problem is hypersomnia (daytime sleepiness) rather than insomnia, you should definitely consult with a sleep clinic, as this may be an indication of several potentially dangerous sleep disorders, such as sleep apnea and narcolepsy.

If your spouse complains about your loud snoring, has noticed pauses in your breathing during sleep, and you wake up in the morning with headaches, all these symptoms may indicate that you have sleep apnea, a breathing disorder occurring exclusively during sleep. A person with sleep apnea may stop breathing 200 or 300 times in a single night, yet be totally unaware of it. The most direct consequence of sleep apnea is chronic sleep fragmentation, which leads to severe difficulty in staying awake during the day.

If you wake up with cramps in your calves at night, or your bed partner has noted leg jerks during your sleep, you may suffer from a condition called periodic leg movements during sleep. As your leg twitches, you may wake up repetitively at night but not remember that on the following day. This condition, also called nocturnal myoclonus, can cause you problems maintaining sleep at night or impair your ability to stay awake during the day. It is often accompanied by restless legs at bedtime, a condition characterized by an uncomfortable aching sensation in the calves and by an irresistible urge to move the legs.

The sleep test can yield valuable information for those who suffer from insomnia as well. There is some controversy among sleep experts, however, regarding the need and clinical utility of a sleep test for those with insomnia. Although an overnight sleep evaluation can be a valuable experience, providing the most comprehensive assessment of your sleep disorder, it may not always be necessary. On the other hand, if, after diligently following the treatment program described in this book, you still have problems sleeping at night, you may have some other sleep disorders of which you are unaware and that can be detected only by an overnight sleep evaluation.

There are several other disorders, like chronic nightmares and sleep terrors, that may not require an overnight sleep test but should still be brought to the attention of a sleep disorders specialist. If you or someone in your family suspects any sleep disorders, you should talk to your family doctor about it or call directly a sleep disorders center for a thorough evaluation.

How to Find the Right Place for You

Sleep disorders medicine is a relatively new discipline. Laboratories devoted mostly to sleep research have been around for many years, but it is only recently that clinics have been developed to respond to the needs of thousands of those who suffer from sleep-related disorders. While just 10 to 15 years ago only major teaching hospitals had sleep disorders centers, today almost every medical center has such a clinic. Currently, there are over 300 sleep disorders centers in the United States and Canada that are accredited by the American Sleep Disorders Association and many more free-standing clinics. To get more information about those centers, you may call the American Sleep Disorders Association or the National Sleep Foundation. (See appendix for listing of these and other helpful organizations.) Although specialized sleep clinics require a referral from your doctor, you may be able to make an appointment directly by yourself.

Insomnia is by far the most frequent sleep complaint; paradoxically, the majority of sleep disorders centers specialize in the evaluation and treatment of more medically based disorders, such as sleep apnea. The reason for this paradox is economic; most insurance companies provide coverage for potentially life-threatening disorders, such as sleep apnea or narcolepsy, but are reluctant to reimburse for a sleep study that is performed for insomnia, a disorder that doesn't kill, even though it greatly affects the quality of life.

Few health-care professionals are trained or have the expertise to treat insomnia, especially with nonmedicinal methods. So if your main problem is insomnia, you should ask if there are professionals on the staff who specialize in its treatment. Before you make a self-diagnosis, however, you may still find it useful to undergo a comprehensive sleep evaluation. Sleep specialists are trained in assessing various conditions; if insomnia is the main diagnosis, and appropriate expertise for treatment is not available, you will be referred elsewhere for treatment.

WHAT IS THE COST OF AN OVERNIGHT SLEEP EVALUATION?

The cost of an overnight sleep evaluation varies between $1000 and $1500 a night. This will cover the hospital charges and the professional fees for reading and interpreting the results. At some centers, it may also cover the initial and follow-up office visits. Insurance coverage is variable, depending both on your carrier and specific policy. As a general rule, sleep lab tests conducted for sleep apnea or narcolepsy have much better coverage than those performed for insomnia. The main issue involved is, as always, the determination of the medical necessity of the test. Despite more limited coverage for insomnia, most insurance companies will cover your initial office visit, regardless of diagnosis. Always check with your insurance company beforehand to avoid any unpleasant surprise.

5

The Self-Management Approach

In the next several chapters, you will learn specific strategies to beat insomnia and to regain control of your sleep. Before we get into the specifics of those methods, we'll review the basic philosophy of the self-management approach and outline some ground rules for making the program work for you. There is a brief sketch of each treatment component, along with an outlook of the program's effectiveness.

THE MIND-BODY RELATIONSHIP AND SLEEP

Our lifestyle plays a vital role in how long and how well we live. What we eat, how much we drink, how often we exercise, and whom we are intimate with influence our physical health, above and beyond hereditary factors. Our psychological make-up—coping styles, thinking patterns, and emotional reactions—is equally important in setting up this life-quality–longevity equation. Research into the mind-body connection increasingly finds that stress, anxiety, and depression can make some people more prone to certain diseases and even delay recovery. Conversely, people with a more effective coping style, those who seek information and adopt a problem-solving approach, often heal faster or live longer, even when faced with a terminal disease.

Sleep is a prime example of the relationship between our mind and body. The ease and soundness of our sleep are intimately connected to our emotional and physical well-being. Although there are many potential causes of insomnia, medical and psychological ones (see Chapter 3), your initial appraisal of the problem is critical in determining whether it will be a temporary problem or turn into a chronic one. Self-efficacy, or the belief that one possesses some degree of control over a particular problem and its outcome, is extremely important in one's successful resolution of that problem. For insomniacs, the erroneous belief that sleep is disrupted by something beyond their control, such as a chemical imbalance, leads to a sense of hopelessness and helplessness, further exacerbating the sleeping difficulty.

The basic philosophy of the self-management approach advocated in this program is that you can overcome insomnia by taking an active role in the treatment process. A most important goal is to dismiss the view that you are a victim of a sleep problem and to adopt one in which you are capable of solving or at the very least coping with the problem. Increased knowledge about insomnia and its causes will help you clarify what you can and cannot change. Then you will develop self-management skills to alter behaviors, attitudes, beliefs, and lifestyles that interfere with sound sleep.

TAKING CONTROL OF YOUR DESTINY

Insomniacs who feel helpless and out of control often turn to sleeping pills in a frantic attempt to cure their problem, only to find that the medication leads to further feelings of dependency or even an exacerbation of insomnia should they try to come off the medication. Other insomniacs resist the temptation to take sleeping pills, fearing the side effects or short-lived nature of their effectiveness. Whatever their stance, individuals with chronic insomnia say things like "There's nothing that can be done about my sleeping problem," or "I've tried everything and nothing seems to help." Indeed, the feeling of being different from others and not being able to control this basic human function can be very distressing. This treatment program offers a way to break the vicious cycle of helplessness and hopelessness.

How does this approach differ from other types of treatment for insomnia? If you previously sought treatment for insomnia, most likely you were prescribed a sleeping pill in the hope that it would "cure" the problem. But the sleeping pill is merely a temporary solution. At times, it may be the only viable alternative, but the fact remains that this intervention does not attempt to uncover the underlying cause of the sleep problem. The individual ends up feeling helpless in relation to sleep, which only leads to a worsening of the problem.

The self-management approach takes the view that you need to be in charge of your own destiny. You don't have to be a victim. The approach is geared toward helping you regain control by teaching you skills to use and ways to cope with and overcome insomnia. The emphasis is not on "curing" insomnia, because an occasional bad night of sleep is the norm rather than the exception. The belief that you will never have another bad night's sleep is an unrealistic expectation that will contribute to the perpetuation of the insomnia. The main focus of the program is to teach you skills to minimize the occurrence of sleep difficulties and to help you cope with residual ones, which all of us have to face at one point or another in life.

SOME GROUND RULES OF THE SELF-MANAGEMENT APPROACH

The following are crucial ingredients in any type of self-help program:

1. Commitment and Effort

This sleep therapy program is highly structured and requires effort and diligence. Although the procedures initially appear simple and straightforward, adherence to the entire program is key to a successful outcome. To begin with, you must make a commitment of time. Successful completion of this treatment requires between 6 and 10 weeks, depending on the duration of the disorder, its severity, presence of other medical or psychological problems, and your own motivation. Do not expect a "quick fix" or results in only a week or two. Be skeptical of any insomnia treatment programs claiming overnight success. Your sleeping problem has probably existed for some time, and it will take time to regain control of your sleep. A commitment of a few weeks is actually quite small in comparison with the suffering you have already endured.

2. Support

Next, it is helpful to elicit the support of the important people in your life. This training program may require that you make changes in sleep habits and lifestyle that will affect not only you but your spouse or other members of your household. Helping them to understand these changes will mitigate any resistance on their part and may prove to be extremely helpful in your own adherence to the treatment regimen. For example, many couples enjoy reading or watching TV in bed before turning out their lights for the night. Eliminating that practice may initially be difficult for your bed partner. But if you elicit his or her support beforehand, you will probably find your partner more cooperative. A partner or another member of the household can also be helpful in reminding you about adherence to the procedures. For instance, people who have trouble staying awake in the evening while sitting in an easy chair or lying on the sofa often benefit by a significant other gently nudging them to stay awake. Finally, you will need support and encouragement from your loved ones if you have been using sleeping pills and one of your goals is to come off the medications.

3. Develop a Scientific Attitude

All scientists share one common belief: you can't make assumptions about the effectiveness of a particular treatment, but must base your beliefs on the evidence or outcome. It is important to look at the facts and try out procedures before you make a snap decision about whether they will work for you. The procedures recommended in this program have been carefully researched and stand up under scientific study. Give them an honest try and then, after a prescribed period of time, evaluate whether or not they are working for you. Be inquiring, as a scientist is. Try to understand what factors interfere with your sleep. Examine what you do, think, or feel before a poor night's sleep, and how that is different from what precedes a good one. Allow yourself to be educated about healthy sleep practices. Question the effects on your sleep of negative thinking. Don't allow inertia or false assumptions to stand in the way of your sleep.

Table 5.1. GOAL-SETTING FORM

Current Sleep Pattern (Before Treatment)

Based on a typical night's sleep (i.e., past 2 weeks), how long does it take you to fall asleep after turning the lights off?	_____ minutes
How many times do you wake up in the middle of the night?	_____ times
How much time do you typically spend awake in the middle of the night? (total duration for all awakenings combined)	_____ minutes
On a typical night, how many hours of sleep do you get?	_____ hours
How many nights per week do you use a sleep aid?	_____ nights

Desired Sleep Pattern (After Completing Treatment)

After turning the lights off, I would like to fall asleep in . . .	_____ minutes
If I still wake up in the middle of the night after treatment, I would like to wake up no more than . . .	_____ times
If I still wake up in the middle of the night after treatment, I would like to be awake for no more than . . .	_____ minutes
If I still wake up too early in the morning, I would like to wake up no more than __ minutes before the desired time.	_____ minutes
I need this much sleep to feel rested and function well during the day and would like to achieve this sleep duration.	_____ hours
I would like to use sleep aids no more than __ nights per week.	_____ nights

4. Setting Realistic Goals

What specifically do you want to change about your sleep? Do you want to fall asleep faster, wake up less frequently or for shorter durations, or sleep longer? Or are you more concerned about waking up too early in the morning or about how you feel during the day? Do you wish to stop using sleeping pills? The important point is that a good night's sleep may have different meanings to different people. Goal setting can help you define more clearly what the problem is and what changes you are seeking.

Before you set goals for your sleep, you must assess what your present sleep is like. You should keep a daily sleep log for at least 1 week, preferably 2, before beginning treatment. Then you can fill out the goal-setting form (Table 5.1). Using the baseline data derived from your two weeks of sleep monitoring, enter the information under the section labeled "Current Sleep Pattern." Next, think about what you would like your sleep to be and enter the information under the section "Desired Sleep Pattern." Remember to be realistic about your goals. Setting goals that are unrealistic or too stringent, such as wanting to fall asleep "as soon as my head hits the pillow" or to sleep "8 hours every night," can lead to frustration and eventually disappointment when you find the goal cannot be met. Also, make sure the goals are your own, not those which someone else wants for you. Finally, remember that the emphasis of this program is not on "curing insomnia"; instead, it is on improving your sleep pattern to a satisfying state and minimizing the frequency and intensity of future sleep difficulties.

5. Self-Monitoring of Sleep

A crucial aspect of this self-management program is the record you keep of your sleep. You do it by recording various sleep parameters in a daily sleep diary (see Table 5.2). The purpose of the sleep diary is threefold. First, you will have accurate information about the frequency and intensity of your sleep problem on a nightly basis instead of trying to recall what went on over the course of a week. By keeping the sleep diary you may notice that your sleep is not as bad as you first thought. Second, it will help you uncover some of the factors associated with a bad night's sleep, as well as with the good ones. Third, the sleep diary data are essential for an evaluation of your progress or lack thereof. A blank diary is provided here. Since you will need 1 diary each week, you should make at least 10 copies of this form.

Table 5.2. SLEEP DIARY

Name: _____

Week: _____ to _____

	Example	Mon	Tue
1. Yesterday, I napped from __ to __ (note the times of all naps).	1:50 to 2:30 pm		
2. Yesterday, I took __ mg of medication and/or __ oz of alcohol as sleep aid.	Ambien 5 mg		
3. Last night, I went to bed and turned the lights off at __ o'clock.	11:15		
4. After turning the lights off, I fell asleep in __ minutes.	40 min		
5. My sleep was interrupted __ times (specify number of nighttime awakenings).	3		
6. My sleep was interrupted for __ minutes (specify duration of each awakening).	10 5 45		
7. This morning, I woke up at __ o'clock (note time of last awakening).	6:15		
8. This morning, I got out of bed at __ o'clock (specify the time).	6:40		
9. When I got up this morning I felt __ (1 = exhausted 5 = refreshed).	2		
10. Overall, my sleep last night was __ (1 =very restless 5 = very sound).	3		

Wed	Thu	Fri	Sat	Sun

In order to better understand your insomnia problem and monitor your progress during treatment, you will need to collect some important information about your sleep pattern. Soon after you get up in the morning, please answer all 10 questions on the sleep diary. It is important that you complete this diary every morning. It may be difficult to estimate how long it takes to fall asleep or how long you are awake at night. Please remember, however, that we want only your best estimates. Many people are concerned about the accuracy of their judgments in recording their sleep parameters. Some try to be absolutely accurate and begin checking the clock so that they can document every minute. Obviously, becoming overly concerned about accuracy and watching the clock can interfere with your sleep. It is not necessary to watch the clock when you keep your sleep diary. The most important thing is to complete the diary every day for the duration of the program. If you forget it one day, however, there is no need to go back; just skip that day. It is best to fill it out in the morning, soon after you arise. Estimate the figures and do not worry about being absolutely accurate. Studies indicate that although people may not judge the figures with complete accuracy when compared with objective measurements from nighttime sleep studies, there is an adequate relationship between subjective and objective measures. Below are some guidelines to help you answer each question. An example is also provided on the diary.

1. *Napping.* Record the beginning and end of any time spent napping from the previous day. This should include all naps, even those which were not intentional (you dozed off in front of the TV for 10 minutes).

2. *Sleep aid.* Include both prescribed and over-the-counter medications, as well as alcohol.

3. *Bedtime.* Record the time you went to bed the night before. If you went to bed at 10:30, read for 45 minutes, and turned the lights off at 11:15, write both times in that space.

4. *Sleep-onset latency.* Provide your best *estimate* of how long it took you to fall asleep after you turned the lights off and intended to go to sleep. If you were unable to sleep and got back out of bed and then went back to bed and fell asleep later, consider sleep latency to be the time between first turning out your lights or attempting to fall asleep and the time you actually fell asleep. Let's say, after turning out your

lights at 11:15 P.M. you were unable to sleep and got out of bed at 11:30 for 30 minutes. You went back to bed and fell asleep within 15 minutes. The total amount of time it took you to fall asleep would be 60 minutes (from 11:15 to 12:15).

5. *Number of awakenings.* Record the number of times you woke after you initially fell asleep.

6. *Duration of awakenings.* Estimate how long you were awake each of those times. This means that if your sleep was interrupted three times, you should have three different numbers in box 6. If this proves impossible to note, then estimate the number of minutes you spent awake for all awakenings combined. This should not include your very last awakening in the morning.

7. *Morning awakening.* Record the very last time you last woke up in the morning; if you woke up at 5:00 but went back to sleep for a brief period (for example, from 6:00 to 6:20), then your last awakening would be 6:20.

8. *Out-of-bed time.* Record the time you actually got out of bed for the day.

9. *Feeling on rising.* Judge how refreshed you felt that morning, using the following 5-point scale: 1 = exhausted; 2 = tired; 3 = average; 4 = rather refreshed; 5 = very refreshed.

10. *Sleep quality.* Rate the overall quality of your sleep using the following 5-point scale: 1 = very restless; 2 = restless; 3 = average quality; 4 = sound; 5 = very sound.

At the end of a week of recording you will need to summarize the data from your diary. A small calculator will come in handy. You can use the summary data form in Table 5.3. In order to calculate summary data across the week, you should record all time in minutes, not hours. Start by recording the dates of the beginning and ending days of the week. Next, compute a nightly average for each sleep variable. Under SOL (sleep onset latency), you will record the average sleep onset latency in minutes by summing up the minutes for each night in question number 4, then dividing this number by the number of nights (usually 7, unless you skipped a night or more of recording). The next item on the summary sheet is WASO (wake after sleep onset). This figure is derived by adding all the times in number 6 of the diary and again dividing by the number of nights. The next item, EMA (early-

Table 5.3. WEEKLY SUMMARY OF SLEEP DIARY
             DATA

Week	Date	SOL	WASO	EMA	TWT	TST	TIB	SE	NA	MED
Before Treatment										
1										
2										
During Treatment										
3										
4										
5										
6										
7										
8										
9										
10										

Note: SOL, sleep-onset latency; WASO, wake after sleep onset; EMA, early-morning awakening; TWT, total wake time (SOL + WASO + EMA); TST, total sleep time; TIB, time in bed; SE, sleep efficiency (TST/TIB × 100%); NA, number of awakenings; MED, number of nights used sleep medications.

morning awakenings), is determined by the difference in minutes between last awakening (no. 7) and arising time (no. 8). Add these figures across the week and divide by the number of nights. TWT (total wake time) is found by adding the average SOL, WASO, and EMA for each night. To determine TST (total sleep time), you must first figure out TIB (time in bed). This is the amount of time elapsed between the time you first went to bed and the time you arose. So if you went to bed at 11:30 P.M. and arose at 6:30 A.M., your TIB for that night would be 420 minutes (7 hrs. × 60 min.). Write this number at the bottom of each column. Again, get the average TIB by adding the nightly TIBs, then dividing by the number of nights recorded in the week. Now you are ready to figure out the TST for each night. Take the TIB for each night and subtract the TWT for that night (the sum of SOL, WASO, and EMA for that night). This is the TST for that night. Add the TSTs for all nights, then divide by the number of nights. Once you have a weekly average TST and TIB, you can figure out the SE (sleep efficiency) by dividing the average TST by the average TIB and multiplying it by 100. This tells you what percentage of your time in bed is spent actually sleeping. A sleep efficiency of 85 percent or better is considered normal.

Record each of the weekly averages of the above sleep parameters on your Summary Data Sheet. This will provide you with a record of your sleep, which you can use for comparison as you go through the training program.

OVERVIEW OF TREATMENT PROGRAM

There are five distinct aspects of this treatment program, each examining a different angle of your insomnia: (1) changing poor sleep habits, (2) revising faulty beliefs and attitudes about sleep, (3) managing daytime stress, (4) maintaining good sleep hygiene, and (5), for long-term users of sleeping pills, eliminating or reducing hypnotic medication use.

After the initial self-assessment and goal setting, the first therapeutic ingredient is to change poor sleep habits. Frequently, insomnia sufferers develop strategies for coping with insomnia and its presumed harmful effects on daytime functioning. They tend to spend an excessive amount of time in bed in an attempt to catch up on lost sleep. They may sleep late into the morning, nap during the day, or go to bed early in the evening in the hope of getting some extra sleep. In fact, their whole sleep schedule may become altered and out of sync with the outside world. Although some of these strategies may help in coping with insomnia on a short-term basis, in the long run the strategies backfire, causing more harm than good. In Chapter 6, we will go over a series of important procedures to follow in helping to eliminate sleep-incompatible activities and to maintain a consistent sleep-wake rhythm. You will be guided in restricting your time in bed in order to help consolidate your sleep over a shorter period of time.

Worrying over lost sleep can lead to emotional upsets and further sleep difficulties. In order to go to sleep you must be worry-free. In Chapter 7, we will see how to assess your beliefs and attitudes about

Table 5.4. THE SEVEN STEPS TO A GOOD NIGHT'S SLEEP

Step 1: Getting Started
Self-assessment
Keeping a sleep log
Setting realistic goals

Step 2: Changing Poor Sleep Habits
Maintaining a consistent sleep-wake rhythm
Curtailing sleep-incompatible activities
Reducing the amount of time spent in bed

Step 3: Thinking Your Way out of Sleeplessness
Revising faulty beliefs and attitudes about sleep
Unrealistic expectations; false attributions

Step 4: Managing Daytime Stress
Learning to relax your mind and body
Changing the stressful situations

Step 5: The Basics of Sleep Hygiene
Caffeine, nicotine, alcohol, exercise
Your bedroom environment: light, noise, room temperature

Step 6: Kicking the Sleeping Pill Habit
A gradual withdrawal program

Step 7: Maintaining Progress over Time
How to deal with setbacks
Preventing relapse

sleep and the consequences of insomnia. You will identify beliefs that are self-defeating and lead to anxiety, thus exacerbating the insomnia. You will get new information to correct false assumptions or misinformation you may have about insomnia and its consequences. You will learn how to substitute healthier, more adaptive thoughts and beliefs for the dysfunctional ones that are contributing to your sleeping problem.

Another important aspect of insomnia treatment involves the effective management of daytime stress. If such stress is keeping you from getting your sleep at night, you will find helpful the stress-management procedures described in Chapter 8—ways to achieve physical and mental relaxation, including techniques like progressive muscle relaxation, meditation, and visual imagery. Other methods, such as time management, assertiveness training, and social support, are also useful in keeping your daytime problems from becoming nighttime ones.

In Chapter 9, we will discuss the basics of sleep hygiene, examining such lifestyle factors as diet, use of caffeine, and exercise, as well as environmental factors, such as the bedroom surroundings, your mattress, light, noise, and room temperature. A series of guidelines to safeguard against their interference with sleep will be outlined.

The final ingredient consists of discontinuing sleeping pills. Although an occasional sleeping pill may be helpful in periods of acute distress—during a crisis or serious medical illness, say—long-term use of hypnotic medications may be counterproductive. A significant percentage of insomniacs are dependent on sleeping medication. They may attempt to discontinue medication because of the stigma they feel it carries or because of side effects, like daytime grogginess or the feeling of being ''doped up.'' Many find that sleeping medications lose their effectiveness after a short period of time, and they either switch to another type or increase their dosage in order to get the same effects they once did. But long-term users typically become frustrated or hopeless when they attempt to withdraw from sleeping medication and find that their insomnia worsens. They often feel they must go back on the sleeping medication in order to sleep. Chapter 11 offers a structured schedule for gradually discontinuing the use of sleeping aids. However, it is important to enlist the help of your prescribing physician in planning the safest withdrawal schedule with minimal risks of medical complications.

These five treatment components may not be equally relevant to your own situation; for example, if you do not use sleep medication, then you can skip the chapter addressing that issue. In general, the two modules dealing with changing poor sleep habits and revising your beliefs and attitudes about sleep are the most important to insomnia sufferers. You can also alter the sequence with which you implement each treatment component; again, changing sleep habits and beliefs and attitudes may be the most important step in the overall treatment of your insomnia. If, however, you're someone who is addicted to caffeine, you may need to examine the basics of sleep hygiene first.

Is This Approach for You?

There are many factors that may cause insomnia, and some may require medical attention. Some sleep disorders other than insomnia may also require evaluation by a sleep specialist. If you have any doubt, or if you show symptoms of any of the disorders described in Chapters 4 and 12, you would benefit by having a thorough evaluation by a professional at a sleep disorders center.

If you are free of the symptoms mentioned above and of complicating medical or psychiatric disorders, you are a good candidate for self-treatment. The next thing to assess, then, is your motivation. Any self-help program requires discipline. In fact, much of the treatment depends on your willingness to carry out the instructions. If you are the type who needs to be constantly prodded or pushed into taking care of yourself, this approach may not be for you; it requires that you take charge of your life and control your own destiny. Relying on others to check up on you or nag you will defeat the purpose of the program. However, social support and encouragement are important aspects of the program and of your eventual success. If you can adopt an inquisitive, scientific attitude and are willing to apply diligence and effort, this program is for you. You may also implement the program with the guidance of a professional mental health therapist. You may benefit from working with a therapist specifically trained in cognitive-behavioral therapy.

How Effective Is This Treatment?

The treatment program has been well-researched, in our sleep clinic as well as in several other centers throughout the world, and has been proven effective in the management of chronic insomnia. For example, we have tested the clinical procedures described in this program with several hundred patients who suffered from various forms of insomnia. The results showed that between 70 percent and 80 percent of treated patients improved their sleep patterns after an average of six to twelve weeks of treatment. One third of the patients became "good sleepers" by the end of treatment, whereas a similar proportion showed significant improvement without becoming good sleepers. Before treatment, the typical patient was taking close to an hour to fall asleep and was awake for an additional hour and a half after initial sleep onset. After treatment, most people were able to fall asleep within 30 minutes and were awake for less than 30 minutes in the middle of the night. Sleep quality was enhanced, and most of the patients were significantly more satisfied with their sleep patterns. More than 50 percent of patients who were regularly using sleep medication before enrolling in our treatment either stopped or substantially reduced their use of sleeping pills. Using a similar non-drug treatment program, other well-known insomnia experts, such as Dr. Peter Hauri at the Mayo Clinic and Dr. Colin Espie at the University of Glasgow in Scotland, have achieved comparable benefits for their patients.

An important aspect of the treatment is that it will help you feel more in control of your sleep and better equipped to cope with any residual sleep difficulties you may encounter even after completing the program. Remember that we are not necessarily aiming to increase your total sleep time, which is generally prolonged by only about half an hour; the main objective is to make your sleep more efficient relative to the amount of time spent in bed. This is achieved by reducing the amount of time it takes you to fall asleep and the amount of time you spend awake during the night; that is, gaining more restful and more satisfying sleep. As a final note, remember that this treatment program is designed as an alternative to the commonly used drug therapies for insomnia. Although drugs may provide rapid sleep improvements, the gains are usually temporary. This drug-free treatment may take a little longer to produce results, but the benefits are long-lasting.

6

Changing Poor Sleep Habits

Most people develop personalized bedtime rituals and sleep habits. Children enjoy bedtime stories and are comforted by soothing objects—a doll, a teddy bear, a special blanket. Adults have sleep rituals, too. After the evening news, you may check the doors, take a last look at the children, turn out the lights, and proceed to the bathroom to wash your face, brush your teeth, take your contact lenses out, and so on. Some can sleep only on a certain side of the bed, in a particular body position, and with a special kind of pillow. Others are very particular about their mattresses and the bedroom environment. Still others may be able to sleep only with ear plugs, eye masks, and white noise in the background. For most people, bedtime routines and rituals are performed automatically and represent strong cues signaling the approach of sleep. There may come a time, however, when all the signals previously conducive to sleep have become associated with apprehension, fears, and sleeplessness. In this chapter, we review how poor sleep habits are learned and how you can change them to beat insomnia.

How Poor Sleep Habits Are Learned, How They Can Be Changed

Chronic insomnia does not develop overnight. As we saw in Chapter 3, it usually follows situational sleep difficulties caused by stress in your job, marriage, finances, or your health. When the stressors fade away, most people resume their normal sleep patterns, but others may have developed negative reactions to stimuli normally conducive to sleep (e.g., bed, bedtime, bedroom). What used to be a place and time for relaxation and sleep is now associated with frustration, anxiety, and sleeplessness, even after the precipitating events have vanished. Over time, a conditioning process leads to a vicious cycle of insomnia, worries, and further sleep disturbances.

A number of poor sleep habits may feed the problem. In response to sleeping difficulties, you naturally try to find a way to cope with them. You may sleep in late in the morning, take naps, or spend extra time in bed in an attempt to compensate for poor sleep at night. Although these practices are excellent coping strategies for dealing with the short-term effects of disrupted sleep, in the long run these same practices may change a situational problem into a persistent one.

As you implement this sleep-training program, you should remember several principles. First, regardless of what triggered your insomnia, psychological and behavioral factors almost always perpetuate it. For example, even if your sleep problem was initially caused by pain, it is very likely that over time such practices as staying in bed too long or worrying about your sleeplessness have become additional causes of the insomnia. Second, it is imperative to tackle directly these maladaptive behaviors in order to get to the heart of your insomnia, even though there may be other contributing factors, such as pain, a hormonal imbalance, or depression. Third, most of these habits are learned and can therefore be unlearned. We will show how you can become a good sleeper by changing some of those lifestyles, behaviors, and habits.

Eight Effective Strategies for Beating Insomnia

There are several steps you can take to modify your sleep habits; a summary is outlined in Table 6.1. These procedures come from two highly effective treatment programs known as stimulus control therapy, designed by Dr. Richard Bootzin, a clinical psychologist at the University of Arizona, and sleep restriction therapy, developed by Dr. Art

Spielman, of the City College of New York. The behavioral regimen is aimed at achieving three objectives:

1. to set the occasion for sleep to occur when desired;
2. to strengthen or renew the association between sleep and its cuing properties—the bed, bedtime, and the bedroom surroundings; and
3. to consolidate sleep over shorter periods of time spent in bed.

To achieve the first goal, prepare yourself adequately before you even think of going to bed; to achieve the second, eliminate activities incompatible with sleep once you are in bedroom surroundings. The basic principles are analogous to those in dealing with a weight problem. Overweight people may develop the habit of eating whenever they feel hungry and wherever that might be. A first step in the self-management of obesity involves restricting yourself to eating only at mealtime and only in the kitchen or a dining area. Likewise, when treating insomnia you must alter the relationship between a particular behavior (sleep) and the stimulus conditions (bed, bedtime, bedroom) controlling it. Because insomnia may be exacerbated by irregular sleep schedules and by too much time spent in bed, the third objective of this program is to maintain a regular sleep-wake schedule and curtail the amount of time you spend in bed. In the remainder of this chapter, each procedure is described, along with its rationale, common obstacles that may crop up along the way, and practical solutions for implementation.

Table 6.1. EIGHT EFFECTIVE STRATEGIES FOR BEATING INSOMNIA

---

1. Allow yourself at least one hour to unwind before bedtime.
2. Develop a pre-sleep ritual.
3. Go to bed only when you are sleepy.
4. If you can't sleep, get out of bed and leave the bedroom.
5. Maintain a regular rising time in the morning.
6. Reserve your bed for sleep and sex only.
7. Do not nap during the day.
8. Restrict the amount of time you spend in bed to the estimated sleep time.

---

1. Allow Yourself At Least One Hour to Unwind Before Bedtime

Use this transitional period to read, watch television, listen to music, or talk with your spouse. As you get closer to bedtime, it is best not to rehash events of the day or plan tomorrow's schedule, as this can create mental stimulation. Set aside another time during the day or early evening to deal with worries and to do problem-solving. If you can't get rid of worries or concerns, it often helps to write them down and plan to deal with them at another time.

John had just landed a job as a sales representative and felt heavy pressure to bring in new customers to his company. He would get home from work around 6:00 or 7:00, eat dinner, and spend time with his family until about 9:00. Once the children were in bed, he went right back to his study to catch up on unfinished business until 11:00 or midnight. By then, his body was exhausted and he could no longer keep his attention focused. His mind, however, remained wired for another hour or so after he went to bed, which naturally prevented him from falling asleep in a reasonable amount of time.

If you are like John, constantly pressed by deadlines and compelled to work until the very last minute before getting into bed, you may need to manage your time differently. We will address this issue in Chapter 8. Meanwhile, you have to set aside at least one hour before bedtime to unwind. Otherwise, it should come as no surprise that your mind is likely to remain at work for some time after you turn out the lights. There is, unfortunately, no switch that you can just turn off to go to sleep. Falling asleep is a gradual process, and failure to allow for a transition period is likely to result in excessive arousal, which will delay the onset of sleep. In a sense, you should prepare yourself for a night's sleep as you would for a journey. You wouldn't just jump into your car and leave, would you?

2. Develop a Pre-Sleep Ritual

It is useful to engage in the same routine every night before you head off for bed. The ritual may involve taking your clothes off and putting pajamas on, washing, brushing teeth, checking the doors, turning out the lights, unfolding the blankets. When practiced regularly, this pre-sleep ritual serves to signal to your mind and body that you are settling down for the night and getting ready to go to sleep. Be careful, however, not to overdo it; you do not want to become rigid to the point that it becomes a compulsive ritual.

Shirley was so concerned that she might not be asleep by 10:30 that her entire evening was spent on preparing for sleep. After getting home from work, preparing dinner, helping her son with his homework, she would take a long warm bath and put on her nightclothes as early as 8:00. She would then settle with a book in her bedroom, waiting and waiting for sleep to come.

3. Go to Bed Only When You Are Sleepy

Insomniacs often start thinking "bedtime" right after dinnertime. To increase the chances of being asleep by the desired time (e.g., 11:00 P.M.) or simply because of boredom, some may go to bed as early as 9:00. Although they may be tired or even exhausted, typically they are not sleepy by that time. So they read, watch TV, listen to music, or rest in bed, hoping these activities will induce sleep. Unfortunately, such practices are counterproductive. If you repeatedly engage in these activities at bedtime, the bed and bedroom surroundings will become cues for wakefulness rather than for sleepiness. Also, when you go to bed too early, you have more time to ponder events of the day, plan the next day's schedule, and worry about your inability to fall asleep. These internal monologues are incompatible with relaxation and are not conducive to sleep. They serve only to cause more apprehension about insomnia and to reinforce the negative association between the bedroom surroundings and sleeplessness. Thus, you should postpone or delay your bedtime until you are sleepy; remember not to confuse fatigue with true sleepiness. Learn to recognize those signs (e.g., yawning, heavy eyelids) suggesting that sleep is imminent.

4. If You Can't Sleep, Get Out of Bed and Leave the Bedroom

When you are unable to fall asleep or return to sleep within 15 to 20 minutes, get up, go to another room, and engage in some quiet activity. You can read, listen to music, watch a movie tape, or practice any similar nonstimulating activity. Wait until sleep is imminent and then go back to bed. Do not sleep on the couch, because this will create an association between sleep and the couch, not sleep and your bed. Initially, you may have to repeat these steps several times throughout the night; it is important that you do so both when unable to fall asleep at bedtime and when you wake up at night and can't return to sleep. It will be difficult and demanding to follow these instructions; however, diligent adherence to the regimen will help you once again to associate your bed and bedroom with getting to sleep *quickly*.

Failure to get out of bed when you are unable to fall asleep is a major impediment to overcoming insomnia. If you are like most poor sleepers, you toss and turn and repeatedly postpone getting out of bed. The underlying belief is that if you keep trying, sleep will eventually come. There may also be some concern that if you do get out of bed, you will be awake for the rest of the night. If nothing else, most of us prefer to stay in bed, assuming that at least we are getting some rest. Nonetheless, the practice of lying in bed while trying harder to go to sleep only exacerbates performance anxiety, frustration, and sleep disturbances. If you truly want to short-circuit this vicious cycle, you should just get up. There is no need to watch the clock, as this alone will keep you awake. When about 20 minutes have passed and you are still awake, you should pull yourself out of this spiraling situation. You may be surprised to find yourself yawning shortly after you get up.

One pitfall in implementing the above instructions is returning to bed too quickly. Often my patients just pace the floor for a few minutes and are eager to return to bed, fearing that if they stay up too long, they will never go back to sleep. But remember that the longer you stay up, the more quickly you will fall asleep when you return to bed.

You may have legitimate concerns that prevent you from following this advice. If it is too cold in the winter months, leave a blanket on the couch. Or you may be afraid that getting up will wake your bed partner, so just ask if he or she has ever been awakened when you got up in the middle of the night. Usually he or she is deeply asleep and doesn't notice it. If this is indeed a problem, consider moving to a different bedroom while you are implementing this program.

5. Maintain a Regular Rising Time in the Morning

Set the alarm clock and get out of bed at approximately the same time every morning, weekdays and weekends, regardless of your bedtime or the amount of sleep you had the previous night. Although it may be tempting to stay in bed later because you haven't slept well the night before, try to maintain a steady sleep schedule. It will help regulate your internal clock and synchronize your sleep-wake rhythm. There is value in the old saying "early to bed and early to rise" when formulating a simple strategy for getting a good night's sleep.

To prevent chronic sleep deprivation, catching up on sleep over the weekends is a fairly common practice. Like napping, it can be a helpful strategy. Insomnia sufferers, however, are particularly vulnerable to its negative consequences. Oversleeping on weekends disrupts the body's natural rhythms and often leads to sleep difficulty on Sunday nights. Although it may be hard to maintain a strict and regular rising time on weekends, particularly when you implement the sleep restriction procedure (rule 8), there are several measures you can take to facilitate the process. The first step is to use an alarm clock even if you usually wake up before the desired rising time. Second, scheduling early social activities or family commitments may increase motivation for getting out of bed early. A spouse or bed partner can also be instrumental in encouraging you to comply with this instruction, though you should ultimately assume the responsibility.

6. Reserve Your Bed for Sleep and Sex Only

Do not read, eat, watch television, listen to the radio, work, or worry in your bed or bedroom either during the day or at night. (Sex is, of course, the exception.) When you engage in these practices in your bedroom, the environment becomes associated with wakefulness rather than with sleepiness. Curtailing these activities in the bedroom will reinforce the associations between that environment and sleep. Just as you may have developed strong associations between the kitchen and hunger or between a particular chair and relaxation, the main objective here is to re-establish a strong connection between sleep and the bedroom surroundings.

For many people, the bedroom is like an office or recreation center.

By choice or by necessity, they tend to organize their entire daily activities within those surroundings. Eating, reading, watching TV, paying the bills, and talking on the phone are just a few examples of sleep-incompatible activities. Some couples tend to solve their problems on the pillow; they use the bedroom and bedtime as a place and time to discuss marital, sexual, or child-rearing difficulties. Because of physical discomfort, some older adults and persons with chronic medical illnesses are also prone to engage in sleep-incompatible activities in their bedroom surroundings.

The main objective here is to let your mind and body know that the bed and bedroom are signals for sleep. It may be argued that many people put themselves to sleep by reading in bed or that many couples have a television set in the bedroom and simply enjoy watching it around bedtime. You should remember, however, that some people are simply more susceptible to the underlying conditioning that develops over time. If you are prone to insomnia and engage in those practices, it is strongly advisable to eliminate them altogether. College students living in a dormitory or people living in bachelor apartments can use a divider between the bed and the rest of the room to minimize those conditioning influences.

7. Do Not Nap During the Day

There is nothing wrong with napping in itself. A short nap can have a powerful revitalizing effect and enhance performance. The afternoon siesta is a custom in Mediterranean and southern countries. Napping is also recommended for those who suffer from a sleep disorder, like narcolepsy. Among insomnia sufferers, however, napping is generally counterproductive. It disrupts the natural sleep-wake rhythm and interferes with nighttime sleep. The longer a person stays awake, the faster he or she will fall asleep when given the opportunity. Thus, when you stay awake all day, the chances are that you will be more sleepy at night.

Although napping is commonly used to cope with the debilitating effects of poor sleep, many insomniacs are simply unable to nap during the day for the same reason that they can't sleep at night. The exception may be when one is simply *not* trying to nap. Poor sleepers usually fall asleep more easily when they are not trying to and are in a non-sleeping environment. For example, you may occasionally doze off in an easy chair while reading the newspaper or watching television. Although you may wake up feeling refreshed, naps, planned or unplanned, do affect nighttime sleep. A late afternoon or evening nap is more detrimental to the following night's sleep than a morning nap. You may remember from Chapter 1 that deep sleep (stages 3–4) is concentrated in the early part of the night, whereas REM sleep is dominant in the second half. A late afternoon or evening nap is made up of more deep sleep, which is borrowed from the beginning of the upcoming night's sleep, whereas the earlier nap is more like a continuation of the previous sleep episode. So a refreshing nap late in the day will have to be paid back by diminished sleep quality during the night.

As with every rule, there are exceptions. First, if you are implementing the sleep restriction program (see rule 8, below), a limited nap is permissible in the early phase, especially if your sleep window is restricted to 5 or 6 hours per night. As nocturnal time in bed is increased, you should gradually eliminate this option. Second, a few insomniacs apparently sleep better at night after a daytime nap, perhaps because their performance anxiety is diminished. Third, napping may not interfere with the sleep of older adults as with their younger counterparts. Finally, if you operate hazardous equipment and daytime sleepiness is overwhelming, pull over and take a nap. For those few exceptions, napping is permissible as long as it is limited to no more than an hour and scheduled before 3:00 P.M. in order to minimize interference with nighttime sleep. To reinforce the properties of the bedroom environment for sleep, it is advisable to nap in bed and at a regular time. It should also be curtailed if no sleep has occurred within 15 to 20 minutes of your getting into bed.

8. Restrict the Amount of Time You Spend in Bed to the Estimated Sleep Time

This procedure, known as sleep restriction, consists of curtailing the amount of time spent in bed as close as possible to the actual amount of sleep. Designed by the psychologist Dr. Art Spielman, the treatment is based on the observation that insomniacs often spend excessive amounts of time in bed. They may go to bed early simply to ensure that they will be asleep by the desired time, stay in bed late in the morning to compensate for sleep loss, or routinely take naps during the day in an attempt to obtain their required share of sleep. Bed rest is one of the most universal strategies for coping with temporary insomnia, and it may indeed provide relief in the short term. Too much time spent in bed, however, may have undesirable effects. In the long run, this coping strategy is ineffective; it leads to more broken or fitful sleep and inevitably perpetuates insomnia. Sleep restriction is designed to circumvent these difficulties. Here is how it works.

First, you need to keep a sleep diary (Table 5.2) for at least one week, preferably two. Second, make a copy of Table 5.3 to use as a summary chart. Calculate your nightly average of (a) total sleep time (TST), (b) time in bed (TIB), which is the time elapsed from lights out to rising time in the morning, and (c) sleep efficiency (SE). Sleep efficiency is computed according to the following formula:

$$\frac{\text{Total Sleep Time (TST)}}{\text{Total Time in Bed (TIB)}} \times 100 = \text{Sleep Efficiency (SE)}$$

Your task is to restrict the amount of time you spend in bed, initially as close as possible to the estimated sleep time, then gradually increasing it until the desired sleep duration is achieved. The following account shows how to implement the procedure.

Steve, a 47-year-old high school teacher, had endured insomnia for the past 10 years. He had trouble with both falling asleep and staying asleep. His sleep diaries kept for 1 week before he was seen in our clinic indicated a usual bedtime of 10:30 P.M. and a rising time around 6:30 A.M., for a nightly average of 8 hours in bed. This may not seem excessive, yet he was taking on average 1 hour to fall asleep and was awake for another hour in the middle of the night. This left him with only 6 hours of sleep out of 8 spent in bed, for a global sleep efficiency of 75 percent (i.e., $^{6}/_{8} \times 100$), which is well below the typical sleep efficiency of 85 to 90 percent considered normal by most experts.

In this example, Steve reports sleeping an average of 6 hours per night out of 8 hours spent in bed, so the initial ''sleep window'' (i.e., from bedtime to rising) is 6 hours. There is no reason for his staying in bed any longer than that, since he is awake then anyway. So Steve decides that he will stay up until midnight and will get up at 6:00 in the morning. This method produces a mild state of sleep deprivation and quickly improves his nighttime sleep. Allowable time in bed is gradually increased, contingent on sleep efficiency (SE). It is increased by 15 to 20 minutes when SE is greater than 85 percent for the previous week, decreased by the same amount of time when SE is below 80 percent, and kept constant when SE falls between 80 to 85 percent. These periodic adjustments are made until an optimal sleep duration is reached. Ideally, the initial sleep window and subsequent changes in allowable TIB are determined according to the data in the sleep diary, which you should keep daily for the duration of the program. In practice, however, it may not always be possible or desirable to follow the rules in rigid fashion. The following guidelines can be used in implementing sleep restriction:

a. Time in bed (TIB) should not be reduced to fewer than 5 hours per night, regardless of how poor sleep efficiency is. Although the goal is to produce a mild state of sleep deprivation, further reductions may impair performance on your job and cause you to fall asleep at inappropriate times or places during the day. If you have a job that is potentially dangerous to yourself or others, you must be careful in implementing this procedure. Do not use it if you are a truck driver and have trouble staying awake at the wheel.

b. Sleep restriction involves a specific sleep window rather than a mandatory amount of time spent in bed. Even though you are allowed 6 hours per night in bed, the actual TIB may be less if you have to comply with the other rule of getting out of bed when you are unable to fall asleep within 20 minutes (rule 4).

c. The specific SE criteria used to modify allowable TIB can also be altered according to your circumstances. For example, if your sleep window was shrunk to the limit initially, you could simply add 15 to 20 minutes on a weekly basis. In this scenario, TIB is gradually increased, regardless of whether SE reached a specified level for the previous week. Likewise, although changes in allowable TIB are usually made on a weekly basis, you may make more frequent changes if your SE consistently exceeds 90 percent for several (five) consecutive days. Be careful, however, not to increase TIB too quickly, as this may just take you back to the old pattern.

d. You have control over selecting either your bedtime or rising time. For example, if the sleep window is set at 5 hours a night, you may choose to go to bed at 11:00 P.M., 12:00, or 1:00 A.M. However, this schedule will automatically set your rising time 5 hours later (i.e., 4:00, 5:00, or 6:00 A.M.). As a rule, it is preferable to alter the time of retiring and keep your rising time fairly stable.

e. What if you just can't stay awake until you are supposed to? This is a good sign. When stimulus control instructions (rules 3–7) are combined with sleep restriction, a double standard is applied. You have to postpone bedtime until you are sleepy, but even then you should follow the guidelines regarding the prescribed sleep window. For example, if your sleep window dictates a bedtime of midnight, you should not go to bed before that time even though you feel sleepy by 11:00 o'clock. At times, paradoxically, you may need to fight sleepiness in order to comply with your sleep window. Occasionally, postponement of bedtime may backfire. A person may be very sleepy at 11:00 P.M. but become wide awake at the prescribed bedtime of midnight. This is usually a temporary problem, which can help you recognize your true sleepiness level.

The idea of decreasing your time in bed, when the usual practice has been quite the opposite, may seem a somewhat surprising recommendation for treating insomnia. You may even wonder whether you will be able to stay awake until the desired bedtime. It is exactly this shift in the focus of your attention—trying to stay awake when in the past you have been trying to fall asleep—that is likely to remove performance anxiety. The paradox usually produces a quick reversal of sleeplessness into sleepiness.

The main effect of this procedure is to cause a mild state of sleep deprivation, which in turn produces faster sleep onset, improves sleep continuity, and puts you into a deeper sleep. Sleep duration is not necessarily increased, but its efficiency and quality are. A possible side effect in the early stage of treatment is daytime sleepiness. This problem is normal and only temporary. You may also realize after one or two weeks that, even with diminished time spent in bed, you are still able to function quite well during the day.

PUTTING IT ALL TOGETHER

The self-management program is a highly structured regimen that requires time, patience, effort, and practice. The procedures reviewed so far are fairly straightforward, at least on paper. Putting them into practice may be more difficult, and obstacles along the way are to be expected. Strict adherence to all the procedures is essential; you cannot choose only those which seem least painful, because the procedures work together. In the early phase of treatment, the initial reduction of time in bed may override the need for some of the other instructions. For instance, if the sleep window is substantially reduced (e.g., to 5 hours), sleepiness will be compelling enough at bedtime that it may not be necessary for you to get out of bed. As time in bed is increased, the need to follow the other instructions will be greater.

You may find that sleep gets worse the first few nights of practice or that you wake up in the morning feeling more exhausted than usual. Do not get discouraged, as this is normal early on in treatment. Benefits will become more evident with time and repeated practice. The single most important factor in determining whether sleep will improve is the consistency with which you follow the instructions. Individuals who carefully follow our recommendations usually start noticing marked improvement in their sleep patterns after 4 or 5 weeks of practice.

The treatment program may sound more painful than the sleep problem you are trying to overcome. Perhaps, but remember that this is a small price to pay if you have suffered sleep difficulties for months or years. Also, keep in mind that it takes time to integrate any new learning experience. When we first learn to drive a car, we have to think of every single movement—turning the ignition on, adjusting the mirrors, putting the transmission into gear, looking all around, accelerating. Obviously this feels awkward at first. With repeated practice, we come to drive our cars without thinking much about the different maneuvers. The same principles apply to this sleep-training program. At first, it may feel unnatural to stay up until 1:00 A.M. or even miserable to get out of bed in the middle of the night when everyone else in the house is sleeping. Over time, these changes will become easier to implement, and once you have beaten insomnia, you may no longer have to think about any of these practices.

In this chapter we have discussed how poor sleep habits are learned and how they can be changed. The next step in solving the insomnia puzzle is to examine how your beliefs and attitudes about sleep may also be part of the problem, and how you can alter those to get a good night's sleep.

7

Revising Your Beliefs and Attitudes About Sleeplessness

It was only 8:00 P.M., and Cheryl was apprehensive about bedtime, thinking, "After what I went through last night, I really need to get some sleep tonight." When bedtime came, she was determined to get to sleep. But her strong determination back-fired, and she was still wide awake at 2:00 A.M. She kept thinking, "Will I ever go to sleep? How in the world will I get through the day tomorrow? Am I going crazy here?" This anxiety kept her awake until daylight. The next day she called in sick at work and walked into our clinic in a state of panic, fearing she might never be able to sleep again. She had not slept a wink the night before. She thought she had some chemical imbalance and was on the verge of a nervous breakdown if sleep didn't come soon. Her self-confidence was shattered; she truly believed her world was coming apart.

HOW FAULTY THINKING CAN FEED INTO THE VICIOUS CYCLES OF INSOMNIA

Cheryl's case is not a dramatization. A faulty thinking pattern can play this kind of trick on you. The way people think about a given situation can cause emotional upsets and aggravate the underlying problem.

Cheryl felt that losing control of sleep meant she really wasn't in control of anything in her life. Getting to sleep requires a tranquil state of mind. Emotional turmoil is one of the worst enemies of sleep. In turn, your thinking pattern is often the main culprit of emotional upsets.

Imagine for a moment four people caught in traffic on their way to work. They've been stuck in their cars for the last 20 minutes at some construction site on the highway. The first person has been thinking about what will happen if she is late for her 9:00 o'clock scheduled meeting; she becomes very anxious. The second one wonders why in the world he took that road, especially after hearing on the radio that some delays were to be expected; he thinks, ''I'm really stupid,'' and he gets down on himself. The third person just cannot understand how they could do construction work during rush hour; she becomes impatient and angry. The fourth person realizes that he can't do much about changing the situation; he may as well stay calm and cope with it the best he can. He reads his newspaper until he can get on his way to work. This example illustrates how our thinking patterns and reactions to a given situation can bring about different emotions.

When it comes to sleep, there is also an intimate connection between what you think and your emotional state. Sometimes your appraisal of sleeplessness itself can trigger negative emotions—anxiety, frustration, depression—and make the problem worse. Typically, you bring those negative emotions on yourself by the way you interpret or appraise poor sleep (see Table 7.1). You can also refer back to Figure 3.1 to see how a faulty thinking pattern can set off a spiral reaction and feed into the vicious cycle of insomnia: stress, worry about sleep loss and its consequences, attempt to control sleep, performance anxiety, further sleep disturbances, helplessness.

For example, if you panic when sleep won't come and expect the worst to happen the next day, of course you'll remain awake. Worrying during the day about how poorly you slept the night before can also make you apprehensive about the upcoming night. Excessive concern about the consequences of insomnia can feed into this self-fulfilling prophecy. If you view sleeplessness as an indication that your whole life is out of control, the chances are you will feel helpless. And if you think sleep is unpredictable, you may very well become depressed. All these emotions are not conducive to sleep. Unlike the person who stays calm when facing difficulties and evaluates them in terms of extenuating circumstances, someone who fears insomnia and its consequences may be in for a difficult time.

Table 7.1. RELATIONSHIPS BETWEEN THINKING PATTERNS AND EMOTIONS

Situation	Thoughts/Beliefs/ Attitudes	Feelings
Eating breakfast in A.M.	How will I get through the day after such a miserable night.	depressed, helpless
Poor functioning at work	I just can't do my work after a bad night's sleep.	angry, irritable
Watching TV in the evening	I must get some sleep tonight.	anxious or apprehensive
Getting ready for bed	What's the use of going to bed tonight when I know I won't be able to go to sleep?	hopeless, helpless

There are many sources of stress, disappointment, and frustration in our lives that can trigger negative emotions and interfere with sleep. We will talk about dealing with those in the next chapter. Here, the point is that sleeplessness itself can be a source of emotional upset and feed into the problem. In this chapter you will learn how changing your attitudes toward sleep can help you get a more restful night's sleep. Before going any further, take the self-test *Inventory of Beliefs and Attitudes About Sleep* (Table 7.2) to examine the extent to which your own beliefs may be contributing to insomnia. We will use several examples from this questionnaire later in the chapter.

Table 7.2. INVENTORY OF BELIEFS AND ATTITUDES ABOUT SLEEP

A number of statements reflecting people's beliefs and attitudes about sleep are provided below. Please indicate on a scale of 1 to 5 to what extent you agree or disagree with each statement. There is no right or wrong answer.

	Strongly Disagree	Disagree	Neutral	Agree	Strongly Agree
1. I must get 8 hours of sleep to feel refreshed and function well during the day.	1	2	3	4	5
2. Because my bed partner "sleeps like a log," I should be able to do the same.	1	2	3	4	5
3. Without an adequate night's sleep, I can hardly function the next day.	1	2	3	4	5
4. When I feel irritable or tense during the day, it is mostly because I did not sleep well the night before.	1	2	3	4	5
5. My physical appearance shows when I haven't slept well.	1	2	3	4	5
6. I worry that sleepless nights can make me have a "nervous breakdown."	1	2	3	4	5
7. I am concerned that insomnia may have serious consequences on my physical health.	1	2	3	4	5
8. I believe insomnia is essentially the result of a chemical imbalance.	1	2	3	4	5
9. I feel insomnia is basically the result of aging and there isn't much that can be done about it.	1	2	3	4	5
10. I have little ability to manage the negative consequences of disturbed sleep.	1	2	3	4	5
11. I must cancel social, family, occupational obligations after a poor night's sleep.	1	2	3	4	5

	Strongly Disagree	Disagree	Neutral	Agree	Strongly Agree
12. I can't ever predict whether I'll have a good or a poor night's sleep.	1	2	3	4	5
13. I have lost control of my sleep and of my life in general.	1	2	3	4	5
14. Insomnia is ruining my ability to enjoy life and prevents me from doing what I want.	1	2	3	4	5
15. Unless my sleep improves, my whole life will remain miserable.	1	2	3	4	5

RECOGNIZING THE THOUGHT PATTERNS THAT CONTRIBUTE TO SLEEPLESSNESS

Everyone entertains some internal monologue about oneself, external events, and about the future. These self-statements—thoughts, beliefs, expectations, attributions (also called cognitions)—flow through our minds during our waking lives. They have an automatic quality and inconspicuous nature. Each of us has our own style of processing information and interpreting what is going on in our lives and in the world. This information is filtered, and sometimes altered, through our past experience, personality styles, and cognitive errors. Cognitive errors mean the filters that affect how we process information: amplification, catastrophizing, overgeneralization, dichotomous thinking, and selective attention.

Cognitive therapy is a treatment method designed to assist you in re-examining the validity of your beliefs, expectations, and attributions and to help you replace them with more adaptable substitutes. It is essentially a mind-framing technique to correct distorted or twisted thoughts and refocus anxiety-inducing thoughts. The basic premise of this approach in regard to insomnia is that faulty thinking may cause or aggravate sleep disturbances by producing emotional upsets. By chang-

ing erroneous beliefs and the underlying thinking patterns, you alleviate psychological distress and ultimately improve your sleep patterns.

A Three-Step Process

You can re-evaluate the accuracy of your thinking through a simple
three-step process:

(a) identify dysfunctional sleep cognitions,
(b) examine and challenge their validity, and
(c) replace them with more productive substitutes.

Identify dysfunctional sleep cognitions. Uncovering self-defeating
thoughts about sleeplessness is the first step in restoring a more positive frame of mind about sleep. Most people don't pay much attention
to, or are unaware of, the automatic thoughts that run continuously
through their mind. For this reason, they fail to realize how such offenders can produce emotional upsets that feed into their sleep problems. To enhance your awareness and identify counterproductive
thoughts, pay attention and keep a record of these views as they unfold
in your mind during the day, evening, or even at night when you're
staring at the ceiling. The *Inventory of Beliefs and Attitudes About
Sleep* illustrates a number of common beliefs and attitudes entertained
by insomnia sufferers. We will return to these shortly. You can also use
a copy of the form provided in Table 7.3 for recording your thoughts,
beliefs, and attitudes about sleeplessness.

Examine and challenge their validity. Once you have identified specific self-statements, such as those in Tables 7.1 and 7.2, the next step
is to explore their validity. Ask yourself the following questions:
"What is the evidence supporting a particular belief? Is it based on
facts or on perception, perhaps distorted by some filters noted above
(e.g., amplification, overgeneralization). Is there any evidence refuting
that belief?" At this stage, it is essential to step back and put aside
previously held beliefs. You must view certain explanations or interpre-
tations as hypotheses rather than as absolute truths.

Replace erroneous beliefs with more productive substitutes. The
most important step of cognitive therapy is to develop alternative and
more productive substitutions for the dysfunctional thought patterns.

Table 7.3. PERSONAL RECORD OF THOUGHTS, BELIEFS, AND ATTITUDES ABOUT SLEEP

Situation	Thoughts/Beliefs/Attitudes	Feelings

This is best accomplished by the mind-reframing techniques illustrated in the next sections.

A word of caution before you go on. You should bear in mind that this approach is not intended to deny or minimize your sleep difficulties and their impact on your daytime functioning. We certainly don't want to antagonize you with dogmatic statements such as "Nobody needs 8 hours of sleep" or "It's all in your mind." Rather, you are encouraged to confront possibly erroneous beliefs, explore alternative hypotheses, and test their validity. The objective is to place insomnia in a more realistic perspective and short-circuit its self-fulfilling nature. After all, you have nothing to lose at this point. Keep in mind that this approach has been found extremely powerful in treating problems such as depression, anxiety, and insomnia.

1. Keep Your Expectations Realistic

There is a widespread belief that 8 hours of sleep is a "must" if you are to feel refreshed and function well during the day. There is also a natural tendency to compare one's sleep pattern with that of a bed partner who may "sleep like a log." In addition, most people wish they would wake up in the morning feeling completely refreshed and full of energy; they are concerned when such expectations are not met.

Sleep needs vary widely among individuals, and short sleep is not necessarily abnormal. Although the average sleep duration for young adults is between 7.5 and 8 hours per night, some natural "short sleepers" can function quite well with 5 or 6 hours, whereas "long sleepers" may need 9 to 10 hours to feel refreshed. There is simply no "gold standard" that everyone should aim for. Avoid placing undue pressure on yourself to achieve a certain standard, as this will only increase performance anxiety. To determine your optimal sleep duration, experiment with various durations and check how you do the next day. You may already have done this with the sleep restriction procedure discussed in the previous chapter.

There are also individual differences in how fast people fall asleep, how often they wake up, and the overall quality of their sleep. Examine carefully the figures from your sleep diaries (e.g., sleep latency, total sleep time) to decide whether your sleep pattern is abnormal or simply falls at the end of the normal range. If you fall asleep in less than 30 minutes, or wake up once or twice for less than 30 minutes, don't worry about it. Any variation within these values is normal. Even if you take 45 minutes to get to sleep, don't try to force yourself to sleep faster. This simply may be what's right for you.

It is equally important to distinguish insomnia from a sleep pattern that changes due to aging. Some middle-aged and older people become concerned when they no longer sleep through the night without waking up once or twice. The number and duration of awakenings naturally increase with aging, and the amount of deep sleep decreases, resulting in an overall diminished quality of sleep later in life. These changes are not necessarily indicative of insomnia.

If you have a different sleep pattern from your bedmate, that does not mean that you have insomnia. Perhaps you envy your partner, who, night after night, falls asleep as soon as he hits the sack and then sleeps through the night. This is indeed the envy of most insomniacs. Keep in mind that sleep patterns vary from person to person, and can even vary for the same person on different nights. After all, not everyone wears the same shoe size, is the same height, or weighs the same. It is best to avoid comparing your sleep pattern with that of others. There will always be someone who is taller, wealthier, or sleeps better than you. Avoid comparisons and acknowledge these individual differences. You might even turn adversity to advantage by thinking how fortunate you are to have more time available as a result of your lower sleep requirements. Some famous people have led very productive and long lives with as little as 5 or 6 hours of sleep a night. The main message here is that a different or changing sleep pattern is not necessarily abnormal.

2. Don't Blame Sleeplessness for All Your Misfortunes

One of the most common reasons prompting insomnia sufferers to seek professional treatment is not so much the sleep problem itself but its perceived consequences. Many are concerned about the effects of poor sleep on performance, well-being, health, and even on physical appearance. The following examples illustrate some of those concerns:

"Without an adequate night's sleep, I can hardly function the next day."

"When I feel irritable or tense during the day, it is because I haven't slept well the night before."

"I am concerned that insomnia may have serious consequences for my health."

"I look terrible when I've slept poorly."

The underlying assumption is that disrupted sleep is detrimental to daytime functioning, mood, and health. Although there is some validity to this belief, there are also three types of cognitive errors that may distort the reality: magnification of the consequences of insomnia (poor sleep decreases motivation but it does not greatly interfere with performance), misattribution of daytime impairments to sleep (sleeplessness is not responsible for everything that goes wrong at work, at home, and with friends), and excessive worrying about those presumed consequences (insomnia may affect your mood but it is not detrimental to health). Let's examine each of these cognitive errors.

The consequences of prolonged and total sleep deprivation need to be distinguished from those of insomnia. The former can be serious, producing daytime sleepiness and poor performance, whereas those specifically due to insomnia are more circumscribed, affecting primarily mood. Nonetheless, the perceived intensity of the daytime problems is often amplified. Studies using objective measurement show only limited impairment of concentration, memory, and judgment among insomniacs. Initiative and motivation are diminished, but actual performance and alertness remain fairly intact. This may be hard to accept by someone who has had firsthand experience with chronic sleep difficulties. How to explain the differences between perceived and actual deficits? Mood disturbances in the form of irritability, worry, and dysphoria, all of which are common after a sleepless night, can alter your perception of performance. This is similar to the reaction of anxious and depressed individuals who perceive their sleep to be more disrupted than is actually reflected by brain-wave activity. To further illustrate this point, let's take the example of a college professor whom I was treating for a classic case of insomnia. She was very concerned about the quality of her lectures, especially when her sleep had been less than adequate the night before. We designed a small experiment where she asked her students to rate her lectures after a good night's sleep and after a poor night's sleep. To her surprise, the student ratings were excellent in both cases. Even if you feel tired, inefficient, and lethargic, then, the chances are that you may be doing much better than you think. But you have to stop dwelling on those deficits.

Your expectations can also play tricks on you. If after a poor night's sleep you are convinced that you won't be able to concentrate or accomplish much of anything on that day, sure enough, your day will be less than productive. If, on the other hand, you block out memory of that poor night's sleep, you may find yourself functioning surprisingly well.

Sleeplessness is an easy target to blame for things that go wrong during the day, but it may not always be the only culprit. Take a close look and ask yourself the following questions: (a) Do I always experience daytime impairments after a poor night's sleep? (b) Are these daytime consequences always felt with the same intensity? and (c) Is it possible that other factors may also be contributing to these problems? Next, generate alternative hypotheses that may explain the impairments. For example, stressors in other areas of your life (family dissensions, conflicting demands from supervisors) may interfere with your ability to concentrate, your energy level, and with your overall daytime functioning. It may also be that you need to revise your approach to time management, problem-solving, and ways of dealing with people.

We will address those issues in Chapter 8. The main purpose of this exercise is not to deny the presence of some aftereffects of insomnia, but instead to question the evidence of a direct causal relationship between sleep difficulties and daytime sequelae. When you attribute all deficits to sleeplessness, it only adds more pressure to get decent sleep.

In sum, blaming lack of sleep for mood swings, low energy, and poor daytime performance is counterproductive. Most likely, factors that have nothing to do with sleep may also be contributing to those deficits. Examine these other offenders closely and try to deal with them directly. Also, remember that nobody functions at peak every day; there are always diurnal variations in performance, alertness, and mood. Virtually everyone experiences periodic difficulties in coping with daily hassles, though not everyone attributes these problems to disturbed sleep. So be careful; don't blame it all on sleeplessness.

3. Revise Misconceptions About the Causes of Insomnia

Trying to understand the cause of a problem is a healthy approach to solving it. In fact, if you are like most individuals with sleep difficulties, you may have some idea of what brought the problem about. One of the obstacles that often arises, however, is that some of these explanations are external and unidimensional. Examples of such causal attributions include:

"My insomnia is basically the result of a chemical imbalance."
"If only I could get rid of this pain, my sleep would be fine."
"Because I'm getting older, it's normal to have sleep problems."

The underlying assumption for such explanations is that you have little or no control over them; it is only by addressing these biochemical, physical, or aging factors that the sleep problem can be resolved. Although some of the attributions may be valid, they essentially remain outside your reach. Dwelling on them can lead to a sense of helplessness and of being victimized.

Joanne had seen numerous doctors and undergone several blood and hormonal tests, without having a clear response about what was causing her insomnia. Yet she was convinced that there was a chemical imbalance keeping her awake at night. Naturally, she also believed that a sleeping pill was the only way to correct her insomnia. Since she had already been on about half a dozen different medications and was still having sleep problems, she was quite desperate.

Joanne's erroneous belief that sleep was disrupted by something beyond her control, a chemical imbalance, led to a sense of hopelessness and helplessness, which itself exacerbated the sleeping problem. Such exclusive attribution of insomnia to external causes is self-defeating, because you may indeed have little control over them. What you need to do first is distinguish the origins of your sleep problem from the perpetuating factors. Regardless of what triggered it initially, insomnia is almost always maintained over time by psychological factors. In Joanne's case, her insomnia began during menopause and, although she had already been on estrogen replacement therapy for two years, she was still suffering from insomnia. While you need to recognize the influence of precipitating factors and, perhaps, accept the fact you may not be able to change them, it is equally important to explore other potential factors that may be exacerbating the insomnia. In Joanne's case these turned out to be her fear of insomnia, a tendency to catastrophize and to anticipate the worst after a sleepless night, a sense of being victimized, and her poor habits of going to bed too early in the evening and staying in bed too late in the morning. Be willing to carefully examine other potential causes, those you can change.

4. Never Try to Sleep

"When I have trouble sleeping, I should just stay in bed and try harder."
"If I try hard enough, sleep will eventually come."

These show what most people do when sleep won't come; they just try harder. This is the worst mistake you can make, because sleep cannot be achieved on command. You may be able to keep yourself awake, up to a certain point, but you cannot force sleep. Whenever you try too hard to control or accomplish something, the attempt backfires and impairs performance—the classic effect of performance anxiety.

The negative impact of excessive motivation to fall asleep was demonstrated in a study where subjects were told that the faster they fell asleep, the more money they could earn. The amount of money offered among the various participants varied. As expected, the financial incentive induced a strong motivation to get to sleep. Subjects offered more money took longer to fall asleep than those offered a small amount. Two other examples illustrate the role of performance anxiety in insomnia. First, many insomnia sufferers fall asleep when they are not trying to, that is, when watching TV or reading. Second, if you ask good sleepers what they do differently from you to get to sleep, most will tell you they do nothing and don't even think about it.

So if sleep won't come, don't try to force it; that will keep you awake. A useful strategy to deal with performance anxiety is to engage in the opposite behavior you ultimately want to achieve; that is, try to stay awake as long as you can. For many insomnia sufferers, the day they stop trying so hard to control their sleep is the day they regain control of it. Just as you should never try to control sleep, it is better that you not attempt to control your thoughts at night. If you are like most insomniacs, you may at times feel overwhelmed by intrusive, uncontrollable thoughts. This racing of the mind is as much a result of being awake as a cause of wakefulness. Dr. Hauri from the Mayo Clinic points out that trying to control your thoughts is guaranteed to chase sleep away. He suggests that you simply let your thoughts wander. Another useful strategy is to organize the thoughts in separate compartments in your mind or simply to get up, write them down, and say something like "I'll deal with that tomorrow."

5. Do Not Catastrophize After a Poor Night's Sleep

Sometimes worrying turns into catastrophic thinking. Like a chain reaction, there is apprehension in the evening, then performance anxiety at bedtime, and finally a full-blown nocturnal panic attack. Some people are concerned that insomnia may have serious consequences on their physical or mental health; others think that not sleeping well is the worst thing that can happen; still others are sure that insomnia is an indication of loss of control and complete chaos in their lives.

Even if you've been awake for hours or just went through a sleepless night, don't panic! Avoid dramatizing the situation with statements such as "I'll never get through the day tomorrow!" Catastrophizing only makes matters worse. Instead, take a step back and ask yourself,

"What's the worst thing that can happen if I never get to sleep to-night?" You might say, "Sure, I'll be sleepy, but I'll deal with it tomorrow." Or, "I'll just have to rearrange my schedule and stay on the cruise control tomorrow." To "decatastrophize" the situation, always keep in mind that the most predictable consequence of sleeplessness is sleepiness. So if you sleep poorly one night, the chances are you'll be more sleepy the next night. And one good night's sleep is usually enough to put you back in shape. Also, if you fear that insomnia may damage your health, remind yourself that excessive worrying can be more detrimental to health than sleep loss itself.

Faulty appraisal of transient sleep difficulties is a common trigger of chronic insomnia. Disturbed sleep is more likely to be distressing when it is perceived as reflecting a loss of personal control than when it is evaluated as a self-limited problem due to extenuating circumstances. For example, viewing a poor night's sleep as the result of a hectic day at work or family conflicts at home is more adaptive than interpreting it as evidence of your loss of control over the ability to sleep. The latter interpretation may lead to performance anxiety and helplessness, which will aggravate the underlying sleep problem.

The lack of explanation for a sleepless night is often the most distressing aspect of insomnia; it can reinforce the personal conviction that sleep is unpredictable. To enhance your self-confidence, look around and identify the possible causes of insomnia. By carefully reviewing activities, concerns, and worries of the previous day or evening, you will almost always uncover some reasons why your sleep was disturbed that night.

6. Don't Place Too Much Emphasis on Sleep

For some people sleep is the essence of their existence. They come to talk about it the way hungry people talk about food. They plan their social, occupational, and family activities on the quality and duration of their sleep. If sleep is less than adequate on a given night, they call in sick or cancel appointments. Taking time off from work or canceling obligations because of poor sleep may reinforce the idea that you are a victim. Such excessive emphasis on sleep increases pressure on yourself to get a decent night's sleep. It also strengthens the belief that insomnia is destroying your ability to enjoy life. Since sleep is supposed to occupy only a third of your life, ask yourself whether you may not be giving it more importance than it deserves. Don't let insomnia run your life.

7. Develop Some Tolerance to the Effects of Sleep Loss

Instead of dwelling on insomnia and its effects on your life, try the more productive approach of developing some tolerance for sleep loss. Try to go on with your usual routines and planned activities. That's not easy, but it will shift your attention away from sleeplessness; it may even show you that daytime functioning is not entirely dependent on the previous night's sleep. You may want to schedule a pleasant activity after a poor night's sleep to disprove that sleeplessness prevents you from doing what you want to do.

Another useful strategy is to stay on cruise control the next day. This doesn't mean canceling your activities but, rather, rearranging your schedule. First, minimize problem-solving, since everything may seem more complicated or more difficult to handle than it really is. Second, take care of the clerical or physical tasks you have put off for some time; they require less concentration and mental energy than other activities. And third, if you must perform certain demanding tasks, schedule them to coincide with a period when your performance is usually at its best.

Whether or not you have trouble sleeping, life has to go on. Try to develop some tolerance of sleep loss and its sequelae. Although insomnia may indeed diminish the quality of your life, it should not be allowed to control it entirely. The idea is to foster the more productive attitude that you can still function adequately and enjoy life despite sleep difficulties; you are not helpless.

8. Dealing with Setbacks

It may take some time before you regain your sense of self-control over sleep. Even after your sleep pattern has become stabilized, you may experience occasional setbacks. Although complete cure is an ideal goal, the reality is that you may have occasional sleep difficulties even after completing this self-management program. To prevent a relapse, you must come to see these bad nights as either natural or resulting from identifiable causes (stress at work, conflicts with spouse) rather than as evidence of loss of control. Close monitoring of your attitudes is especially useful when it comes to coping with these residual problems after treatment. By changing your appraisal of an occasional poor night's sleep, which virtually everyone experiences at one time or another, you will be able to prevent or short-circuit a relapse into a full-fledged chronic insomnia.

In summary, we all have our own sets of beliefs, expectations, and attributions. Some of them may be valid, but others will prove faulty or maladaptive, and feed into the insomnia problem. Self-imposed pressure to achieve certain sleep standards, faulty assumptions about the causes of insomnia, and excessive concern about its consequences can only make your problem worse. On the other hand, you can think your way out of sleeplessness by revising those beliefs and attitudes.

8

Learning to Relax Your Mind and Body

It's 3:00 A.M., and Steve is wide awake. He's been trying to go back to sleep for the last hour; he keeps looking at the clock as the minutes tick by. How will he handle his busy schedule tomorrow if he doesn't sleep tonight? Steve's body is full of tension; he can hear his heart beating. What's more, his mind is racing and he can't shut it off. He's thinking about his rotten day. He remembers that negative interaction with his boss. He thinks about all that paperwork that he has to complete and wonders how he'll ever get it finished. He even skipped lunch, he was so busy. On the way home, he got stuck in traffic; precious time wasted. And Steve's spouse just doesn't seem to realize that he needs a little time to relax when he gets home. The argument the two of them had about who was going to take the kids to their dentist appointment tomorrow made things even worse. Then he spent the whole evening trying to get caught up on that paperwork but didn't even make a dent in it. He had no time at all to relax today. And now, tomorrow will be here before he knows it, and he's going to be exhausted!

Does this scenario seem familiar? If so, you're not alone. Stress is a fact of life we just can't avoid. Stress can contribute to or exacerbate a host of physical problems, such as headaches, ulcers, and hypertension.

It can also lead to or worsen psychological problems like anxiety, interpersonal differences, anger, and depression. Daytime stress can obviously keep you awake at night. As we saw in Chapter 3, a major life event—the death of a loved one, losing a job, or having a child can precipitate insomnia. A less severe but more common stressor can also trigger or exacerbate difficulties sleeping. Pressure at work, difficulties at home, traffic jams, and financial worries can keep most people awake at night. Excessive and repeated demands made on our physical and mental resources, combined with inadequate means to handle those demands, can produce stressful days and sleepless nights. Sleep deprivation itself then aggravates the situation. In this chapter you will learn self-management strategies to help you cope with daily stressors and hassles that interfere with the quality of your life and with your sleep.

The "Fight or Flight" Response

Society constantly bombards us with demands on our time and patience, from the frustrations of dealing with automated telephone systems and the red tape of bureaucracy, to the hectic pace of the schedules of our families. Stress, however, results in part from our perception of and responses to these external demands. When the situations in the environment are interpreted as threatening, your body reacts with a "fight or flight" response; the muscles become tense, heartbeat and respiration rate accelerate, and the extremities become cold and clammy as blood rushes to the trunk and head. This response is adaptive when the circumstances really are life-threatening or dangerous, as they are during an act of violence or aggression. You must decide whether to fight or run away. However, when such a reaction occurs habitually in normal everyday situations like being late for an appointment or having an argument with a co-worker, the individual becomes exhausted, worn down, or emotionally or physically ill. Research conducted by Richard Lazarus and his colleagues at the University of California at Berkeley has shown that it is the minor but frequent annoyances we experience daily that produce more negative effects on health than do large-scale traumas.

Take a few minutes to answer the stress test below. If you answer *yes* to more than half of the questions, you may be stressed out. You would do yourself a favor to re-examine your lifestyle and priorities. Stress management can help you feel less strain during the day and sleep more soundly at night.

Table 8.1. STRESS TEST

I constantly function under time pressure.

I am often overwhelmed by too many demands placed on me.

I often have to reschedule meetings or request an extension of deadline.

I worry a great deal about family, work, health, or finances.

I get easily irritated by co-workers.

I am impatient with other people.

I tend to interrupt other people before they are finished talking.

I find it difficult to keep focused on one task.

I get easily fatigued, mentally and physically.

I suffer from physical ailments such as insomnia, tension headaches, upset stomach.

I have a hard time relaxing and enjoying life.

It is hard for me to let go of work when I get home.

It is difficult for me to schedule pleasant time and activities with family and friends.

People with chronic sleep difficulties do not necessarily experience more frequent or more stressful life events than good sleepers. Their response to those events, however, may be less adaptive. Insomniacs do not cope effectively with daily hassles. Also, it takes them longer to recuperate and to slow down their physiological and emotional activation systems after an unpleasant event. When bedtime arrives, these people may still be physically or emotionally tense, which naturally interferes with their sleep.

How Should You Manage Stress in Your Life?

There are numerous stress management strategies that range from taking a hot bath, to taking a cruise in the Caribbean, to methods inspired by Oriental medicines—acupuncture, massage, herbal potions. Their cost and effectiveness vary a great deal. In this section, we review a sampling of practical and effective methods to keep stress at bay. These methods are designed to (1) reduce your physiological and mental response to stress, (2) alter your appraisal (thoughts, beliefs, attributions) of the situation perceived as stressful, and (3) change or eliminate the circumstances that elicit your stress reactions. Now, let's take a look at some of the techniques for reducing stress in each of these areas.

Deep Breathing

Believe it or not, the very act of breathing may create stress in you. As part of the "fight or flight" reaction, the individual begins to breathe more shallowly and rapidly. This acceleration in breathing helps prepare the person to flee or to fight back by supplying the muscles with increased oxygen, which fuels the cells. As the cells "burn" the oxygen, carbon dioxide (CO_2) is given off as a waste product, which, in turn, is pumped back into the bloodstream. The CO_2 then is expelled through the lungs. A problem occurs, however, when the individual feels threatened and experiences the "fight or flight" response but does not actually engage in increased activity. This is what happens with most everyday stress in our lives. It is then that the delicate balance in the body between oxygen and carbon dioxide gets disrupted, causing problems like improper breathing leading to dizziness, heart palpitations or chest pain, numbness in hands and feet, and fear or anxiety.

Have you ever noticed how peaceful a sleeping baby looks? You can see his little tummy gently moving up and down as he breathes. Abdominal breathing is the body's natural response when it is completely relaxed. When we breathe, we can take air into three sections of the lungs: the lower lungs, resulting in movement of the diaphragm and abdomen, the mid-lungs, resulting in movement in the chest, and the upper lungs, causing a heaving of the shoulders. The diaphragm is the most important muscle to learn to relax. Many adults have forgotten how to breathe deeply from the lower lungs and instead use quick, shallow breathing of the upper chest, which is more appropriate for physical exertion. Learning to breathe deeply from your abdomen can help you to relax and let go of tension in your muscles during the day as well as at bedtime. Here is how to do it.

Get in a comfortable position and place one hand on your abdomen and the other on the top of your chest. Inhale slowly and deeply through your nose. Try to bring the air down all the way to the bottom of your lungs. You should feel the hand on your abdomen gently move. If the hand on your chest moves first, you are still breathing too shallowly. Inhale and exhale until you feel the hand on your abdomen move. If you are unable to get the air into the bottom of your lungs, lie down with a book on your abdomen. See if you can get the book to move as you breathe in deeply. When you have learned to breathe from the lower lungs, practice that breathing for a few minutes several times a day. You may find it helpful to count silently 1000, 1001, 1002 as you inhale through your nose, then 1003, 1004, 1005 as you exhale through your mouth. Pause for one second before beginning again. As you focus on your breathing, feel your body relax. As you continue to breathe deeply, tell your body to relax more and more deeply. Use diaphragmatic breathing any time you feel yourself becoming tense: while driving a car, getting stuck in traffic, when you find yourself upset over negative thoughts, or when you are unable to sleep at night.

Muscle Relaxation

Most people are unaware of the tension they carry in their bodies as a result of the "fight or flight" reaction to stressful situations. The first step in reducing bodily tension is to develop awareness of that tension as it builds up in the muscles; the sooner you catch it, the more effective you will be at controlling it.

Progressive Muscle Relaxation (PMR) is a deep muscle relaxation technique developed by Dr. Edmond Jacobson in 1929. It is the most commonly used method of relaxation applied to stress-related problems such as insomnia, tension headaches, and gastrointestinal problems. In many ways, relaxation is to psychologists what aspirin is to physicians. PMR involves alternately tensing and relaxing muscle groups. You can easily learn the technique, but you must practice it on a daily basis, preferably twice a day for about 20 minutes each session. Make sure to unplug the telephone and let everyone else in the house know that you will not be available for the next 20 minutes. After a week or two of practice, you can begin to shorten the exercises by consolidating muscle groups. With diligent practice, you can train your body to relax automatically when you give yourself the cue ''Relax'' as you begin to notice tension building up. The following is an abbreviated list of some of the major muscle groups involved in PMR:

1. Hands and arms;
2. Forehead, scalp, eyes, and nose;
3. Lower cheeks, mouth, lips, jaw, and chin;
4. Neck and throat;
5. Shoulders, chest, and upper back;
6. Abdomen and lower back;
7. Buttocks;
8. Feet and legs.

Instructions. It is important to learn PMR at a time when you are not feeling particularly tense or stressed so that you can mobilize your energy and concentrate more efficiently on developing this new skill. Begin by getting in a comfortable position, loosening your collar, belt, shoes, and so on. You may lie down if you wish; if you sit up, pick a comfortable, straight-backed chair. For the sake of brevity, these instructions will assume that you are in an upright position, but you may change the instructions to fit your pose. Keep your feet flat on the floor with your legs uncrossed. Put your arms and hands at your side or on the arms of the chair. You will need first to read the following script several times to become familiar with the basic procedures. You can then close your eyes and focus on your breathing. With each breath, let your body relax more and more. When you start to feel relaxed, begin the tensing-relaxing exercises. For all the muscle groups, tensing should last about 5 seconds and relaxing should last about 20 seconds. You should tense the muscles enough to be uncomfortable but not so hard that it is painful. The sequence is (1) tense, (2) scan, (3) relax, and (4) enjoy the pleasant feeling.

Start with your dominant *hand and arm*. Make a fist. At the same time, tense the muscles in the forearm and upper arm. Feel the biceps grow hard and tight under your skin. Hold the tension. Notice what the muscles feel like when they are tense and tight. Now, relax the muscles. Let your arm sink down into the chair, relaxing more and more deeply. Let your fingers gently uncurl. Feel your fingers spreading out, becoming longer. Let all the muscles become smooth and relaxed. Notice how heavy and warm your arm feels. Notice how different the muscles feel now that they are relaxed. Repeat the tensing and relaxing with the dominant hand and arm. Now move to the nondominant side, and repeat twice by tensing and holding, then releasing and relaxing.

Now turn your attention to the upper part of your head. Wrinkle your *forehead,* as if in a frown. Feel your scalp tighten. Shut your eyes as tight as possible. Flare your nostrils. Feel the tension across your forehead and eyebrows. Notice the tension in your eyes and across your cheeks and nose. Pay attention to what it feels like when these muscles are tensed. Relax! Let go of the tension. Let your forehead become smooth. Let your eyelids relax. Feel your eyelids become droopy. Let your nostrils return to a resting position. Feel a sense of warmth traveling down over your scalp, over your eyes, cheeks, and nose. Enjoy the sensation of relaxation. Repeat tensing and relaxing the upper part of your head.

Move to the lower half. Clench your *teeth* tightly together but be careful not to clench so hard that it hurts. Thrust your tongue to the roof of your mouth. Close your lips and pull your mouth back. Notice the tension in your jaw and mouth. Then let go. Relax. Unclench your teeth. Relax your jaw. Let your lips part slightly. Repeat the exercise with the lower half of your head. Stop and experience the sense of relaxation traveling up your fingertips and arms, flowing down over your forehead, eyes, nose, cheeks, mouth, and jaws. Appreciate the feeling of relaxation.

Moving down to your *neck,* press your head as far back as it will go. Feel the muscles in your throat straining and pulling. Hold on to the tension, then relax. Let your head drift back to an upright position. It should feel very relaxed, as if it were perching on top of your neck, being gently pulled up by an invisible hot-air balloon. Repeat the tensing and relaxing; then bring your head forward until your chin touches your chest. Feel the tightness running down the back of your neck into your shoulders. Notice how it feels when these muscles are tensed. Then relax. Bring your head back to an upright position. Feel the muscles become smooth and relaxed. Feel the tension drain away. Repeat.

Bring your *shoulders* up to your ears. Feel the muscles in your shoulders and upper back grow tense and tight. Push back with your shoulders and feel the tension across your chest. Feel the muscles contract in your upper back between the shoulder blades. Relax. Let your shoulders drift back down to a resting position. Feel the space between your shoulder blades growing wider. Feel your shoulders drifting down farther and farther. Repeat.

Moving down to the *abdomen,* pull in your stomach while you inhale in your upper chest. Hold your breath and feel the tightened abdominal muscles. Then exhale and fill your abdominal cavity with air, letting your abdomen push out slightly. Continue to breathe slowly and deeply, feeling all of the muscles in the abdomen relax. Repeat the tensing and relaxing in the abdomen.

Move to the *buttocks* and tighten them. Hold the tension. Then relax. Feel your body sinking down into the chair, becoming more and more relaxed. Repeat.

Now, tense the muscles in your dominant *foot and leg* by pressing your heel down on the floor and pulling your toes up toward the ceiling. Feel the tension running from your toes up over your foot and up through your shin, calf, and thigh. Feel the muscles straining and pulling. Notice the tension. Then relax. Let your whole foot return slowly to the floor. Let the muscles smooth out. Feel your calf relax. And your leg, heavy and warm, melting down into the seat of the chair. Repeat, then switch to the nondominant leg, and do the tensing and relaxing two times.

Now you have finished tensing the various parts of your body. Feel the sense of relaxation throughout your body. Check the various areas to see if you are carrying tension anywhere. If you find any part of your body holding on to tension, just let it go and relax. Check your hands and arms, check your forehead, eyes, nose, mouth, and jaw. Relax.

Scan your neck and shoulders and relax the muscles. Your back and chest. Let go of any tension. Check your abdomen. Let the air gently fill your abdomen as you take slow, deep breaths. Check your buttocks and relax them. Check your legs, thighs, calves, and feet. Take a moment to appreciate the feeling of relaxation throughout your body. Then count backward from 3 to 1 and open your eyes, feeling relaxed and refreshed. Three, two, one, and open your eyes. Congratulate yourself on a job well done.

Table 8.2. RELAXATION DIARY

Day	Time	Stress/Tension Before	Level After	Comments
[Example]	11:45 A.M.	9	4	Felt time pressure
	10:45 P.M.	7	2	Worried about next day
Monday				
Tuesday				
Wednesday				
Thursday				
Friday				
Saturday				
Sunday				

It is important to keep a record or daily log of your relaxation exercises. You can make a copy of Table 8.2 and record the time and each day that you practice relaxation. Also rate your level of tension and relaxation in the following way. Before beginning the relaxation exercises each day, rate how relaxed or tense you feel, on a scale of 1 to 10, with 1 being completely relaxed and 10 being extremely tense and tight. After completing the exercises, rate your level of relaxation again. After you have practiced PMR for about two weeks and your ratings indicate that you feel more relaxed, you can begin to shorten the PMR exercises. One way to do this is by grouping more muscles together. For instance, you may want to group all the muscles in the upper part of your body, tensing and relaxing at the same time hand and arm, shoulders, chest, and upper back. You can also group together all of the muscles in the head and face. The abdominal muscles and buttocks can be grouped, followed by a grouping of the muscles in the leg and foot. Another way to shorten the exercises is to tense and relax both arms at the same time. You may also exercise both legs at the same time.

When you become adept at PMR, you may want to omit the tensing and concentrate only on relaxing the muscles. Tell yourself to relax a particular muscle group. Eventually, you may be able to tell your body to relax and find that you become more relaxed simply by hearing yourself say the word. At this point, you will have conditioned your body to relax on cue. It will be possible now to use this cue to help yourself relax in high-stress situations. Always remember to check your body for tension and use the cue for focal areas that tend to hold tension.

For some people the tensing of the muscles can be distracting rather than relaxing; for those who suffer from arthritis it may even be painful. If this is a problem for you, you might find relaxing of muscles alone, that is, without the tensing component, to be more helpful.

Visual Imagery

Instead of focusing on the somatic sensation resulting from muscle relaxation, some stress-reduction methods focus on imagery to achieve a state of deep mental and physical relaxation. Here is a guided imagery exercise you can try. Or you can make up your own with the images that are most soothing for you.

A Day at the Beach: *Get in a comfortable position, close your eyes, and focus on your breathing. Take slow, deep breaths, filling your abdomen and letting the air gently rise up through your lungs. Feel your body become more and more relaxed. Now imagine yourself walking down a path between two soft white sand dunes. In the distance you can see the ocean. The sea grass gently swishes against your legs as you make your way down the path. Now find yourself on a long, deserted beach. The sand is gleaming white and you see the heat gently rising up from it. Feel the warm sand beneath your bare feet. The day is clear and the sun is shining brightly. You can feel the rays of the sun on your back, penetrating your body, filling you with its warmth. Be aware now of the sounds of the day. Hear the vibrant crash of the waves upon the shore, and the gulls calling out to one another in the distance. Now, walking to the edge of the beach, feel the cool wet sand below your feet. With each crash of the waves upon the shore, you feel yourself letting go of your tension more and more. With each receding wave that pulls the sand from under your feet, you feel your tension slipping away. The warmth of the sun fills you with peace and joy, and the ocean pulls the tension away. This is a perfect day. This is a perfect place. You can come back here whenever you feel tense or distressed. Say goodbye now to the ocean and thank it for taking away your tension. Thank the sun for its relaxing rays. Find your way back up the path and back to this room. Open your eyes and notice how relaxed you feel.*

Many people find it easier to induce a state of relaxation by use of the imagination than by willing themselves to relax through somatic focusing. Several additional methods of imagery for reducing tension are discussed in the excellent book *The Relaxation and Stress Reduction Workbook,* by Davis, Eshelman, and McKay. One such technique involves visualizing your tension as a color and a shape, then changing it to another color and shape. After you have done this, you push the second shape and color away until it is out of your awareness. In another visualization you can imagine your body filled with a particular color that represents your tension. As you imagine the color changing to one that symbolizes deep relaxation and inner peace, you may experience a physical sensation of relaxation as well.

Self-Hypnosis

Hypnotic relaxation can be an effective method for managing stress. Alpha waves are present during a hypnotic trance. These same waves are characteristic of the transitory relaxed period that acts as a bridge between wakefulness and deeper sleep. One technique for self-hypnotic induction involves fixing the eyes on a small point or dot on the ceiling that is above and behind the field of vision. Fixing on a candle or another object also works well. Begin the self-hypnotic induction by getting into a comfortable position. While fixing your eyes on the object or spot, suggest to yourself that your eyelids are growing heavy, that little weights are attached to them, drawing them down. Feel your eyelids growing heavier and heavier. You are having trouble keeping them open. You can no longer hold them open.

As you continue with this form of auto-suggestion, choose a word to say when your eyelids close, a word that you find relaxing. Repeat this word slowly as your eyelids close. Eventually, as you practice, this word alone may be sufficient to induce a trance. With your eyes closed, tell yourself to become more and more relaxed. Imagine going down— a flight of stairs, an elevator, or a tunnel. Tell yourself you are going deeper and deeper. Tell yourself you can come up out of the trance whenever you want to. You can ascend the stairs or elevator, counting backward as you go. Tell yourself to awaken, feeling relaxed and at peace.

While it is beyond the scope of this chapter to explore fully self-hypnotic procedures, this exercise is one you should find helpful. For more detailed information, you should consult a psychologist especially trained in hypnotherapy.

Meditation

Meditation is a mental exercise that can slow down the body's metabolism and respiration rate and increase alpha brain waves, those present in deeply relaxed states. Meditation can also help alleviate muscle tension and anxiety; it has been used to help people quit smoking, manage stress, and conquer insomnia. The goal of meditation is to gain control over your attention through the uncritical focusing on one object. In a world where people are constantly bombarded with stimulation, meditation can help you to focus on what is most important, thus becoming less distracted by the meaningless things or situations that often cause us stress. To learn how to meditate, find a quiet place. Get into a comfortable position and relax your muscles, but in a passive way. You may choose to focus your attention on either a physical object or a repeated word or sound. Breathe regularly. Do not attempt to alter your breathing pattern. If you have chosen to focus on a word or sound, repeat it silently to yourself with each breath you inhale and exhale. For example, repeat in your mind the word "one" when you inhale and "two" when you exhale. If you chose to focus on an object, hold the object (a candle, a rock, or a piece of jewelry) so that you can easily see it. You may want to turn it or stroke it to bring it fully into your visual and tactile senses. Experience the object as completely as you can. Regardless of whether you focus on an object, sound, or word, do not try to control your thoughts. As thoughts enter your mind, let them pass through as you continue to focus on your word or sound. Do not scold yourself if you find yourself distracted by thoughts. Simply let go of them and refocus your attention. Do not try to evaluate your performance. It is not important. Instead, adopt a passive, open attitude. Continue to meditate for about 20 minutes; then open your eyes or stop focusing on your object. When you stop meditating, give your body a few minutes to readjust before going about your day.

A Few Words of Caution

To get the full benefit of any relaxation procedure, you must practice it regularly. If you find excuses for not practicing, such as being too busy, then you are probably one of those most in need of it! Find a quiet place and a time when you are unlikely to be disrupted. Rehearse for at least two weeks during the day before using the procedure at bedtime; it may keep you awake if you are not yet skilled at it.

Although you need to be consistent, don't overdo it! Trying too hard to relax can, paradoxically, lead to performance anxiety. Just be patient with yourself; if after 2 to 4 weeks of diligent practice, you feel it is not helping, it may simply not be for you. Not everyone is a good candidate for relaxation-based interventions. For example, hypnosis is most effective for people with a high level of suggestibility.

Audiotapes of relaxation, imagery, and self-hypnosis are commercially available; you can buy one to help you in the initial training phase. In the long run, however, you should be able to use the skills without having to rely on tapes. The ultimate goal is to develop self-control and have those coping skills readily available when you need them. Last, remember that no relaxation procedure is a quick fix or a miracle cure for stress. These methods should be seen as skills or tools to help you keep stress manageable and make sleep more restful.

CHANGING THOUGHTS OR ATTRIBUTIONS THAT LEAD TO STRESS

Why do people experience the "fight or flight" response in relation to nonthreatening, everyday situations? The answer is that our thoughts about the situation are what determine whether we have a stress reaction, and emotional reactions (stress, anxiety, or depression) are partly shaped by our perception of the world, of ourselves, and of the future. The mind is constantly at work, interpreting situations and silently giving us feedback about them. Sometimes we are conscious of this mental feedback, but more often it is at least partially out of our awareness. Dr. Aaron T. Beck, a psychiatrist and pioneer of cognitive therapy, calls these silent messages "automatic thoughts." Often, the automatic thoughts we send ourselves are negative and distorted, lessening our sense of self-esteem and impairing our relationships with others.

Take the following example. You see two of your co-workers talking together over lunch. You sit down at the table and they immediately become silent. You can interpret this situation in several ways. You may think, "I can tell they don't like me, because they won't share what they were talking about." In other words, you interpret their silence as a threat to your relationship and your self-esteem. This thought may lead to feelings of hurt or anger, resulting in your pulling back from them or holding a grudge. Later in the day, you may become aware of physical problems—a stomachache or headache. You may be irritable and snap at other co-workers. There is another way to interpret the same event, though. When you see your co-workers abruptly ending their conversation, you may think, "They must be sharing something confidential that doesn't concern me. They have a lot of integrity." This interpretation does not threaten your self-esteem and you don't feel stressed by the situation.

One important way to manage stress in your life is to change the perception that a situation is threatening. To do so, you must become aware of the thoughts you have about a situation that lead to negative feelings and reactions. If you are not accustomed to paying attention to your self-talk, you may have to work backward from the negative feelings to the thoughts that caused them. So, when you have already reacted to a situation and are feeling angry or upset, take a step back and ask yourself, "What am I telling myself about this situation?" With practice, you will eventually begin to identify stress-producing thoughts before you have a full-blown stress reaction. After you are able to identify the thoughts that lead to negative feelings or reactions, you must begin to evaluate the validity of these automatic self-statements. Do a reality check. Ask others how they would interpret the situation. Experiment with looking at the situation from other perspectives. Beck talks about cognitive errors or ways our thinking can go awry in processing information. Try to catch yourself making any of the following types of cognitive errors:

1. Overgeneralization (evidence drawn from one example or experience that is erroneously applied to other situations);
2. All-or-nothing thinking (categorizing as either-or, black-or-white thinking);
3. Catastrophizing (imagining the worst that could happen or ballooning what could happen to extreme proportions);
4. Selective attention (focusing only on the negative to the exclusion of the positive);
5. Personalization (interpreting an event or circumstance as indicative of a negative aspect of self or a slight to self);
6. Labeling (turning an example of one behavior into a negative characteristic of the person or self).

We saw in Chapter 7 how those same cognitive errors can feed into the vicious cycle of insomnia, emotional upset, and further sleep disturbances. It is also easy to see how such faulty thinking may cause someone to become stressed or depressed. Often our negative or distorted thoughts about a situation come about as a result of our unrealistic expectations about the situation or about others. "Shoulds" and "musts" result in our dictating rigid standards of behavior for ourselves and other people. Failure to live up to these rigid standards can result in our feeling hurt, angry, or disappointed. Dr. Albert Ellis, father of rational emotive therapy, maintains that there are ten basic irrational beliefs that lead to negative thinking. Look at these statements and try to identify those which seem valid to you.

1. It is an absolute necessity for an adult to have love and approval from peers, family, and friends.

2. You must be unfailingly competent and almost perfect in all you undertake.

3. Certain people are evil, wicked, and villainous and should be punished.

4. It is horrible when people and things are not the way you would like them to be.

5. External events cause most human misery—people simply react as events trigger their emotions.

6. You should feel fear or anxiety about anything that is unknown, uncertain, or potentially dangerous.

7. It is easier to avoid than to face life's difficulties and responsibilities.

8. You need someone stronger or greater than yourself to rely on.

9. The past has a lot to do with determining the present.

10. Happiness can be achieved by inaction, passivity, and endless leisure.

After you are able to identify irrational beliefs or cognitive errors in your thinking, you will need to change these thoughts by substituting ones that will lead to more positive emotions about yourself and your outside world. Do not become discouraged if your first attempts to change your thinking do not lead to more positive reactions. Thought substitution requires much practice. Sometimes it is helpful to write the adaptive thoughts to given situations on index cards and tape them up in a place where you can easily see them. For example, you may find yourself often becoming stressed by other peoples' demands on you, either at work or at home, due to their lack of planning. For instance, the popular slogan "An emergency on your part does not constitute one on mine" can be left on your desk or taped to the refrigerator to remind you that you don't need to rescue others all the time. Given time and practice, you may find that you are automatically substituting adaptive thoughts for the former maladaptive ones. And, most important, you will begin to notice that you are not as stressed out as you once were.

ELIMINATING THE STRESSFUL SITUATION

A third way to deal with stress is to cut it off at the pass. In other words, get rid of the situations that result in stress. Think about your life for a moment. What situations are stressful? Is it the hectic pace of life, your unsatisfying job, or people who call on the phone and upset you? Sometimes attempts to eliminate stress by reinterpreting the situation are not successful because some situations are inherently stress-producing. If you find there are particular things that chronically cause you to react negatively, think about whether you can eliminate or change the circumstances. Here are some ways to do this:

1. Develop Effective Problem-Solving Skills

When you are faced with a stressful situation, you need to (a) identify the situation causing the stress, (b) explore all potential solutions, (c) examine the pros and cons of each solution, (d) implement the chosen solution(s), and (e) evaluate the outcome. By adopting a systematic strategy to problem-solving, whether at work, at home, or in dealing with loved ones, you will reduce your stress level and improve your relationships with others. You will also quite likely improve your performance.

2. Set Priorities and Manage Your Time

In today's culture, with its hectic pace, it is important to plan your time rather than let your time plan you. Steven Covey, author of the national best seller *The 7 Habits of Highly Effective People,* sees time management as divided into four quadrants. In the top left quadrant are activities that are urgent and important—crises, pressing problems, or deadline-driven projects. Activities in the bottom left quadrant are urgent but not important—interruptions, unimportant phone calls, some unimportant meetings. In the bottom right quadrant are activities that are not urgent and not important—busywork, time wasters, and unnecessary paperwork. In the top right quadrant are activities that are not urgent but are important. Here we see relationship building, recognizing or developing new opportunities, planning, goal setting, and recreation. People who are poor managers of time usually engage primarily in activities in the left quadrants or lower right quadrant. They spend their time either putting out brushfires—handling emergencies—or in meaningless activities that leave little time for the big jobs that most need doing. These people spend little time in preventive activities that build relationships and help them determine where they want to go in life. Covey says that letting yourself be habitually driven by problems, crises, or deadlines can result in stress and burn-out. Time spent in unimportant activities, urgent or not, results in irresponsibility and ineffectiveness. But setting your priorities to include some activities in the prevention quadrant can result in a sense of vision and purpose, the feeling of being in control, and, ultimately, fewer crises or "fires" to put out. Additional time-management strategies include the following: make a list of things to do or a plan with operational goals, schedule some uninterrupted time every day, find an easy way to start or begin with the basics, take one step at a time, break down difficult tasks into more manageable ones, postpone self-evaluation, and just do it!

3. Learn to Delegate

Many people feel that to get the job done right, they have to do it themselves. This attitude results in their feeling overburdened and alone, and it leaves them little time for the more important preventive, vision-setting, or relationship-building activities. Being able to trust others enough to give them some of your responsibilities can relieve the burden. Delegating also encourages others to learn new skills and take on new responsibilities. True delegating involves explaining to others what outcomes you'd like to see, then letting them go about achieving the outcome in the ways they see fit. Feeling the need to control the methods or oversee the entire process can be frustrating and leave you with no more free time than you originally had.

4. Be Assertive

Much stress results from our being unable to say *no* to demands made on our time. You may be asked to sit on too many committees, watch other people's children, or cover for co-workers. As a result, you feel out of control and taken advantage of. You do not get your own needs satisfied. Whatever the unrealistic demand, being able to assert yourself and say *no* can be very freeing. However, it's important to differentiate between behavior that is passive, assertive, and aggressive. Self-assertion means being able to express your own needs without hurting others in the process. If you find that you are experiencing stress because it's difficult to say *no* or get your own needs met, you may benefit from a self-help book or group on assertiveness training.

We discussed in Chapter 3 the relationship between assertiveness and sleep difficulties. In my own clinical experience, I have noted how insomnia sufferers are intrinsically kind people. By this I mean that they often are people who would go out of their way to please others, who are more concerned with pleasing others than themselves. Good sleepers, on the other hand, are generally more assertive in expressing their needs and standing up for their rights. And they go to bed with a more free mind and sleep more soundly. Conversely, the lack of assertiveness may result in bedtime worries about what might have been done differently and in doing a lot of "second guessing." Naturally, these internal monologues interfere with sleep.

5. Express Anger in Adaptive Ways

Much stress results from not being able to express anger in a non-threatening way. The two maladaptive types are those who express anger in belligerent or blaming ways and those who hold it in, letting it brew inside. Some "gunnysack," holding in their anger until, triggered by some inconsequential matter, the gunnysack is dumped and the anger comes spewing forth. Expressing anger in nonaggressive ways is a form of self-assertion. Express anger adaptively by making "I" statements rather than blaming or name-calling. Focus on the circumstance you want to change rather than those attributes you find disagreeable. Conflict-resolution skills can also help you deal more effectively with your anger. The first step in conflict resolution involves active listening. Paraphrasing what your opponent says can make him feel he's being heard. Next, you and your opponent should look at alternative solutions in a brainstorming session. Evaluate each proposed solution until all involved can agree on one.

6. Reward Yourself and Take Time to Enjoy Life

The old maxim "All work and no play makes Jack a dull boy" has a great deal of truth to it. Take a minute to evaluate the way you spend your time. You may want to monitor a week for this exercise, writing down your activities hour by hour throughout the week. Now, rate your activities as pleasurable, unpleasurable, or neutral. What proportion of your week was spent on unpleasant activities? How many times in the week did you have experiences you really enjoyed? If you find that most of your time is spent on tasks you consider drudgery, it's no wonder you're feeling stress. Next, make a list of activities that you find enjoyable or exciting. Schedule some of these activities for the following week. Pleasurable activities or small gifts may also be scheduled as rewards for working hard. It is especially important to give yourself time to unwind at the end of a long day. If you work right up until you go to bed, you can expect to have trouble turning your mind off. Plan to spend at least an hour before retiring for the night in doing something that is low-key yet enjoyable.

7. Take Care of Your Body

Most experts in stress management agree that not taking care of yourself physically can result in additional stress. Two ways to take care of your body are through proper nutrition and exercise. Proper nutrition involves a balanced diet with daily selections from the four major food groups. Although the size of servings may vary according to age, weight, and gender, your diet should include more fruits and vegetables and bread or grain products than dairy and meat, poultry or protein products. Fats, sugars, and items high in sodium should be carefully monitored. Vitamins are important in the management of stress. The secretion of cortisol, the stress hormone produced by the adrenal cortex, calls for the use of vitamins. Chronic stress can deplete the B-complex vitamins and vitamin C. Also, substances containing caffeine, such as coffee, tea, some soft drinks, and chocolate, are all central nervous system stimulants and produce stresslike responses. Eliminating cigarettes and avoiding alcohol or using it in moderation can also help to control stress. Exercise is important not only in helping to control weight but also in controlling stress. Aerobic exercise involves sustained (20 minutes or more per workout) rhythmic activity of the large motor muscles and includes running or jogging, dancing, swimming, fast-paced walking, and bicycling. Aerobic exercise improves the functioning of the lungs and circulatory system, enhances the production of red blood cells in the marrow, helps maintain normal blood pressure and a lower pulse rate, and increases energy and endurance. Exercise also strengthens muscles and bones. Before you begin an exercise program, it is important to have a physical examination and get your physician's OK. Other types of exercise that are of low impact and low intensity are yoga, isotonic, and isometrics. These exercises involve stretching or contracting of muscles, and will increase muscle strength and flexibility. Yoga can also be combined with meditation. Whatever type of exercise you choose, remember these helpful hints: (a) never exercise too close to bedtime, (b) start gradually and build up, (c) make sure you practice warm-up and cool-down exercises, (d) set goals for yourself and monitor your progress, (e) exercise at least three times per week, (f) reward yourself for following through with praise but not with food, and (g) most of all, choose a form of exercise that is enjoyable. Forcing yourself to exercise in a mode that is unpleasant can only result in greater stress.

8. Find a Supportive Social Network

Social support appears to be a factor in preventing or ameliorating stress. In our highly mobile, fast-paced culture, many people find themselves cut off from family and friends. Facing our problems alone can in itself be stressful. Supportive people who care about us can make all the difference in the world in how we handle stress, so make time in your life to find people who share your values, who will be there when you need to talk, and who will celebrate your joys and share your sorrows. There is no substitute for people, especially in a world of high-tech communication that makes it increasingly feasible to put in an 8-hour day of work at home at the computer terminal.

This chapter has focused on the relationship of stress and insomnia and outlined three important ways to deal with stress in your daily life. The first, that of decreasing your physiological and mental responses to stress, explored such practices as deep breathing, muscle relaxation, meditation, visual imagery, and self-hypnosis. The second suggestion was to change your perception that an event is stressful. Here, we looked at ways to identify maladaptive thoughts that result in emotional upsets and to substitute more adaptive thoughts. The last strategy for handling stress consisted of changing or eliminating the circumstances or events that lead to a stress reaction. Some ways to alter the stressful situation included setting boundaries and learning to say *no,* managing time and setting priorities, delegating, expressing anger in adaptive ways, rewarding yourself, taking time to unwind at the end of the day, taking care of your body, and finding a supportive social network.

We are not disconnected from our daytime activities when we sleep. Stress is often what keeps people from getting restful sleep. It is unrealistic to expect that you can lead a stress-filled life during the day and suddenly be free of worry at night. Coping with stress effectively during the day can only lead to a more peaceful sleep.

9

The Basics of Good Sleep Hygiene

Sleep is affected by a host of lifestyle factors: diet, exercise, alcohol use; and by environmental factors: mattress, ambient temperature, noise, light. In this chapter, you will learn how health practices and environmental influences can promote or interfere with a good night's sleep. First, to examine your sleep hygiene quotient, please take a moment to answer the following quiz.

Table 9.1. SLEEP HYGIENE QUOTIENT

Do you consume caffeine in the evening?
Do you smoke near bedtime or when waking at night?
Do you have a nightcap at bedtime to help you unwind?
Do you eat a heavy meal before going to bed?
Do you snack in the middle of the night?
Do you exercise vigorously near bedtime?
Does your bedroom look like a battlefield?
Is your mattress too hard or too soft?
Is your room temperature too hot or too cold?
Is noise keeping you awake at night?
Is there any light coming through at night?

Like most insomniacs, you are probably aware of the effect of those factors on your sleep. Nonetheless, surveys show that while insomniacs are well informed about sleep hygiene, many feel immune from those influences and actually engage in more unhealthy practices than good sleepers do. So if you answered in the affirmative to any of those questions, read this chapter to learn more about the basics of proper sleep hygiene. Table 9.2 sets out in brief some guidelines to follow that will improve your sleep hygiene practices and help you find the way to get your rest. More detailed information is provided in the rest of the chapter.

Table 9.2. SLEEP HYGIENE GUIDELINES

- Caffeine is a stimulant and should be discontinued 4 to 6 hours before bedtime.
- Nicotine is a stimulant; avoid smoking around bedtime and when waking at night.
- Alcohol is a depressant; it may help induce sleep but will disrupt it later in the night.
- A light snack may help, but don't eat a heavy meal just before bedtime.
- Regular exercise may deepen sleep, but avoid exercising too close to bedtime, as that can be overstimulating.
- Keep your bedroom neat and clean; select a comfortable mattress.
- Avoid extreme room temperature; keep the temperature moderate.
- And keep your bedroom quiet and darkened.

1. Caffeine: Discontinue Caffeine Use 4 to 6 Hours Before Bedtime

Caffeine is the most widely used drug in our society. It is a central nervous system stimulant and is often used by people who want to stay awake. Naturally, if it is taken close to bedtime, it produces light and fitful sleep. Depending on its preparation, one cup of coffee contains anywhere between 75 mg (instant) and 200 mg (brewed) of caffeine, which is virtually absent from decaffeinated beverages. Caffeine reaches its maximum concentration in the bloodstream between 15 and 45 minutes of intake. It takes about 3 hours to eliminate half of the caffeine from one's system, although this may vary from one person to another. Caffeine consumed an hour before bedtime, then, may delay the onset of sleep and, when ingested right at bedtime, may interrupt sleep during the night. Moderate daytime consumption is unlikely to affect nighttime sleep, but its heavy use throughout the day may be followed by evening withdrawal symptoms, like headaches, which can delay the onset of sleep.

Most people are aware of the stimulating effects of caffeine and are careful not to use it after dinnertime. As I am often reminded in my practice, however, we should not overlook the stimulating effects of those friendly companions of our evening television viewing—soft drinks, iced tea, chocolate. A recent patient of mine, Jack, was quick to claim that he never drank coffee after dinner; yet when I asked about other caffeine-containing products, he acknowledged drinking Pepsi almost continuously throughout the evening, with one or two bars of chocolate candy. Caffeine is present not only in coffee, it is contained in smaller amounts in tea, cocoa, chocolate, several soft drinks (Pepsi, Coke), and various over-the-counter medications (anorectic, allergy, and cold remedies). Bedtime use of these products can have the same detrimental effect on nocturnal sleep as coffee.

Sensitivity to and tolerance of caffeine products varies among individuals and may have different effects on sleep. Increased tolerance may explain why some habitual caffeine consumers do not complain of sleep difficulties. Insomniacs may be more sensitive to its stimulating effects because of a greater predisposition to hyperarousal. In general, however, caffeine used near bedtime will disrupt the quality of sleep in everyone, even in those who claim it has no effect on their sleep.

2. Nicotine: Avoid Smoking Around Bedtime and on Waking at Night

Nicotine is a central nervous system stimulant and has much the same effect on sleep as caffeine. Although smokers may experience a sense of relaxation, the overall effect of nicotine is one of stimulation. A small dose of nicotine may produce a mild and very brief period of sedation, but with a higher dose, this state is rapidly replaced by in-

creased heart rate, blood pressure, and similar effects caused by stimulants. The result is one of physical and mental activation which is
incompatible with sleep. The stimulating effects of caffeine and nicotine when combined are particularly detrimental to sleep.

Surveys and laboratory studies do confirm the association between
smoking and sleep difficulties. Smokers, particularly those who go
through more than one pack a day, take longer to fall asleep and then
wake up more frequently than nonsmokers or those who smoke less
than a pack a day. Excessive smoking around bedtime may lead to
conditioned awakenings in the night. Heavy smokers, for example, find
that their first thought on waking in the middle of the night is of
reaching for a cigarette. Sleep interruptions may become conditioned
to nicotine withdrawal.

If you are a smoker, the best advice, obviously, is to quit smoking
altogether. Research studies have shown that smoking cessation improves sleep patterns, despite some initial withdrawal symptoms during
the day. For those who can't or won't kick the habit, it is particularly
important to reduce the rate of smoking in the few hours before bedtime. Also, they should avoid smoking when they wake at night; this
may prevent conditioning those awakenings to nicotine withdrawal
symptoms.

3. Alcohol: Be Careful with the Nightcap; It May Help Induce
Sleep but Will Disrupt It Later in the Night

Unlike caffeine and nicotine, alcohol is a central nervous system depressant. It is nonetheless the most likely substance to cause sleep
disruption. A nightcap may help tense individuals to relax and to fall
asleep more quickly, but as the effect wears off, sleep becomes lighter
and more fitful. Alcohol is metabolized at approximately the rate of
one drink per hour, and the withdrawal effects may persist for 2 to 4
hours, even after the alcohol level in the blood has returned to zero.
Thus, even a moderate and socially acceptable amount of alcohol between dinner and bedtime is likely to disrupt nocturnal sleep. As the
alcohol is metabolized, the body experiences withdrawal symptoms,
which in turn cause restless sleep and nighttime awakenings. A shot of
liquor in the middle of the night in an attempt to return to sleep is

followed by the same withdrawal symptoms later in the night or on waking in the morning.

Alcohol consumed around bedtime will reduce REM sleep in the early part of the night, which will be followed by a rebound (increase amount) in the latter part of the night. Excessive REM activity may in turn trigger nightmares. Early morning awakenings are also quite common after even moderate alcohol intake the night before. Thus, the net result is one of diminished duration and quality of sleep.

The effects of chronic alcohol abuse are particularly detrimental to sleep. Following a binge, sleep is initially deeper, but during withdrawal there is a marked reduction of deep sleep and a slight decrease of REM sleep. Behavioral and dietary factors often interact with alcohol abuse in altering the sleep-wake cycles. Even during abstinence, sleep may remain disturbed for extensive periods of time and may precipitate a relapse. Although sleep therapy can be helpful in preventing a relapse, treatment should be directed at the underlying substance-abuse problem.

For social drinkers and those using an occasional nightcap as a sleeping aid, the best advice is to avoid alcohol or switch to nonalcoholic beverages for 4 to 6 hours before bedtime. A drink may help anxious individuals to relax at bedtime, but the overall effect is of diminished sleep quality and duration. Alcohol should never be mixed with sleeping pills; it aggravates all the effects just described. Alcohol also makes snoring worse, and if you have symptoms of sleep apnea, alcohol's use at bedtime is strictly contraindicated, as it will aggravate the underlying breathing disorder.

4. Diet: A Light Snack at Bedtime May Promote Sleep, but Don't Overeat

Food intake can promote sleep, but the timing, type of food, and the amount of caloric intake are important mediating factors of this effect. For example, a light snack at bedtime seems to promote sleep. A heavy meal at bedtime is counterproductive; it makes your digestive system work overtime. You should avoid the following foods around bedtime: spicy foods, peanuts, beans, and most raw fruits and vegetables, which can cause gas. Avoid snacks in the middle of the night, because nighttime awakenings may become conditioned to hunger. Excessive fluid intake in the evening may interrupt your sleep with the need to urinate.

Are there some specific food nutrients that promote sleep? There has been little research on the effects of various foods and dietary habits on sleep. Aside from clinical observations that a meal high in carbohydrates (bread, cheese, crackers) promotes sleepiness and one high in protein enhances alertness, claims that certain diets promote sleep are for the most part unsubstantiated. What about a glass of milk? We've all heard about this old recipe and most parents have witnessed first-hand the soothing effect of milk on a baby at bedtime. L-tryptophan, a natural amino acid, is found in milk and in many other dairy products. Its concentration, along with the neurotransmitter serotonin, is increased during sleep. Theoretically, then, it should promote sleep. Research studies, however, give mixed results, some reporting improved sleep while others showed no effects, even with a much larger quantity than what is naturally available in a glass of milk. The specific effects of other dairy products (ice cream, yogurt, cheese) on sleep is uncertain, as their tryptophan content is much lower than that in concentrated pills. Until several years ago L-tryptophan was available in most health food stores. However, several cases of eosinophilia, a blood disease associated with an increase of white blood cells, were linked to use of this food supplement. Investigations by the Food and Drug Administration (FDA) and the Centers for Disease Control later concluded that the disease was not caused by L-tryptophan, but rather, resulted from contaminating substances inadvertently introduced into the manufacturing process of a few batches of the food supplement. Nevertheless, the FDA has maintained its recommendation to withdraw from the market L-tryptophan in concentrated pills.

Drastic changes in diet and body weight can disrupt normal sleep patterns. Weight loss is accompanied by short and broken sleep, while weight gain is associated with long and continuous sleep. Sleep difficulties can be quite severe in patients with such eating disorders as anorexia or bulimia, although it is not clear whether those changes are related to nutritional deficiencies, the mood disturbances that often accompany eating disorders, or both. Sleep usually improves after weight gain.

In summary, a light snack with a nonalcoholic and noncaffeinated beverage before bedtime may foster sleep in some individuals. Although it is best to avoid going to bed hungry, a heavy meal before bedtime is to be avoided. Do not eat snacks in the middle of the night, as in the long run hunger may trigger night wakings through a conditioning process. Lessen your fluid intake in the evening. Excessive liquid intake may lead to the need to urinate and problems returning to sleep, a potential problem especially in older adults, who are more prone to bladder problems and who may already use diuretics (fluid pills) to control blood pressure.

5. Exercise: Regular Aerobic Exercise May Deepen Sleep; Avoid Vigorous Exercise Within Two Hours of Bedtime

The benefits of regular aerobic exercise on physical fitness and emotional well-being are established. Exercise can also improve your sleep. Running, swimming, skiing or any energy-expending activity promotes deep sleep. We saw in Chapter 1 that sleep serves several functions; deep sleep (stages 3–4) is primarily involved in recovery from fatigue and the restoration of physical energy.

Three factors seem to affect the relationship between physical exercise and sleep—one's physical fitness, the timing of the activity in relation to the sleep period, and the amount of energy expended. Regular aerobic exercise by physically fit individuals improves sleep patterns; specifically, it increases the amount of deep sleep. Sustained and vigorous exercise in untrained or sedentary individuals has the opposite effect; it produces lighter and more restless sleep. The timing of exercise in relation to the sleep period is equally important. Exercising just before bedtime has a stimulating effect and therefore interferes with the onset of sleep. Conversely, physical exercise in the morning may have little effect on nighttime sleep because it is too long before the sleep period. The best time to exercise is in late afternoon or early evening. The sleep benefits come from the "cooling off" of the body that occurs a few hours after you exercise. You can achieve a similar effect by taking a hot bath in the evening. The rebound cooling following active (exercise) or passive (hot bath) body heating is conducive to sleep, and this cooling occurs earlier with passive than with active heating, which explains in part why vigorous exercise should not be done within 3 or 4 hours of bedtime, whereas a hot bath can be taken up to 2 hours before bedtime. Finally, the amount of energy expenditure is an important variable in the relation between exercise and sleep. Running a marathon affects sleep differently from jogging for 30 minutes. Strenuous exercise is likely to disrupt sleep the following night even in the most fit individual.

In summary, there are two basic recommendations. First, avoid vigorous exercise too close to bedtime, and, second, enroll in a regular exercise program in late afternoon or early evening to improve sleep as well as to enhance your physical and emotional well-being. Although exercise alone is rarely sufficient to cure chronic and severe insomnia, regular physical activity can be a useful adjunct to the other methods you have learned thus far. For poor and good sleepers alike, it is an excellent method of stress reduction.

6. Designing the Right Niche: Bedroom, Mattress, Pillow, and Sheets

If you've been struggling to get your rest, don't overlook the obvious. Just as good job surroundings are conducive to your working efficiently, so you should have the right set-up to sleep soundly at night.

The bedroom itself should be inviting. Try to create an environment with a pleasant and soporific effect. Use colors that are relaxing and soothing; avoid those which are stimulating or depressing. Keep the furniture to a minimum. Don't make an office or a recreation field of your bedroom; reserve it for sleep and sexual activity so that it will serve as a strong cue for those activities only. Keep your bedroom neat and clean. Make your bed in the morning rather than at bedtime; it will provide you with a sense of order and control in your life. You may need an alarm clock but avoid watching it at night, as it will only keep you awake longer. If you can hear the tick of the clock, cover it with a blanket or a pillow.

There is a great deal of variation in individuals' preferences for personal items such as mattresses, pillows, and sheets. What matters the most is that you find what gives you the most comfort. If you wake up with night sweats, use light sheets made of cool fabrics. A mattress that is too hard may cause sleep difficulties in those with arthritis, whereas one that is too soft may present problems for those with lower back pain. You may be able to correct an excessively soft mattress by placing boards beneath it, though you may have to replace it altogether. There is no evidence showing sleep to be any different on a waterbed than on a regular mattress. Again, this is a matter of personal preference.

7. Keep Your Bedroom Temperature Comfortable

Avoid an excessively hot or cold, dry or humid environment. Although there is no ideal room temperature for everyone, an extreme temperature interferes with normal sleep. A hot room (above 24 C or 75 F) increases night wakings, reduces REM and deep sleep, causes more body movements, and diminishes the overall quality of sleep. Sleep difficulties are less frequently associated with cold temperature, although a room temperature below 12 C (54 F) is sometimes associated with unpleasant and emotional dreams. If there is no thermostat in your bedroom, you can adjust the temperature with blankets or a fan or air-conditioning.

Your body temperature is also associated with sleep propensity. We saw in Chapter 1 that body temperature varies by about 2 degrees Fahrenheit from peak to bottom throughout the 24-hour sleep-wake cycle. It is lowest in the early morning hours, when the sleep propensity is highest; it begins rising shortly after, to reach a peak in late morning or early afternoon, when alertness is at its maximum. Sleep scientists have observed that the body temperature of insomniacs tends to remain more elevated throughout the 24-hour period than that of good sleepers. This finding is consistent with insomniacs' reports of feeling hot at night, so it is best to keep your bedroom well ventilated and preferably on the cool side.

8. Avoid Excessive Noise and Light

Noise from a snoring bedmate, a neighbor's barking dog, or street traffic can be both annoying and disruptive to your sleep. You might nudge your spouse or move to the couch, but such a solution is only temporary. We will see in Chapter 12 that snoring can be corrected with appropriate surgery. When it comes to the neighbor's dog, you may have to assert yourself the next day to prevent the disturbance from happening again. As for the other sources of outside noise, you can always shield the windows and better insulate your bedroom. In general, the background noise from a fan or specially designed "white noise" device can mask many disruptive sounds. Ear plugs will also significantly reduce the noise level. Although good sleepers may become accustomed to noise, their sleep patterns remain more shallow and light. The awakening threshold is lowest in stage 1 sleep, highest in stages 3–4 sleep, and variable in REM sleep. The kind of auditory stimulus influences this threshold. A new parent will wake up more easily from a crying baby than from street noise. The threshold becomes lower with age, which explains why older adults have more trouble staying asleep than young people. A noise level sufficient to wake up a 70-year-old causes only a temporary shift to light sleep in a 25-year-old. Insomniacs are more sensitive to noise, perhaps because they are already awake or in a lighter sleep, or are simply more aware of their environment.

Lighting conditions can affect sleep in almost anyone; this factor alone explains the high incidence of insomnia in night workers trying to sleep during the day. It is particularly important to have a well-darkened room with window shades that keep out street lights or daylight. The use of eye masks or goggles can also eliminate or reduce undesired illumination.

In this chapter, we have seen how some lifestyle and environmental conditions can have a detrimental effect on nocturnal sleep, and how you can promote a good night's rest through proper sleep hygiene. Although inadequate sleep hygiene is rarely the primary cause of insomnia, it may complicate an existing problem and hinder your efforts at changing other harmful habits, beliefs, and attitudes. It is important, then, to take proper actions to safeguard against interference from these factors, and to integrate the basics of sleep hygiene into the overall treatment program described in this book.

10

Resetting Your Body Clock

Not all forms of insomnia are triggered by stress, anxiety, and emotional turmoil. Some are caused by an internal clock that is simply out of sync with the outside world. There is a misalignment between this biological clock and the desired sleep-wake schedule, or the one regarded as the societal norm. For example, a person may sleep quite well from 3:00 A.M. to 11:00 A.M., or from 8:00 P.M. to 4:00 A.M. Such a condition is called a circadian rhythm disorder, because it is primarily due to the poor timing of the sleep episode within the 24-hour day. Other examples of the condition are caused by rapid time zone changes (jet lag) and shift work. The main difficulty is that the person cannot sleep when she wants to and cannot stay awake when she needs to. In this chapter we review some important principles regulating the body's rhythms, sleep-wake problems associated with irregularities of the biological clock, and ways to reset it.

YOUR BODY'S RHYTHMS

Everyone has a biological clock, an internal timekeeper that regulates several physical and mental functions—sleep-wake cycles, hormone secretion, body temperature, mood, alertness, and productivity. In fact, there may be several clocks regulating each of these functions according to a different cycle. The "master clock," or pacemaker, that keeps them in harmony with each other, is located at the base of the brain, in the hypothalamus (see Chapter 1 for more details).

Our natural tendency to be active during the day and to rest at night is largely determined by the light-dark cycle, which itself is governed by the rotation of the earth over a 24-hour period. Through an intimate connection of nerve cells between the hypothalamus and the retina, the light-sensitive layer at the back of the eye, the amount of daylight exposure sets the timing of sleep and wakefulness. In blind people, this line of communication is short-circuited, resulting in irregular sleep-wake schedules. Cataracts in older people may also confuse their internal clock and interfere with their sleep schedules.

Secretion of the hormone melatonin by the pineal gland is also influenced by the light-dark cycle. Melatonin is secreted when the eyes register darkness; it reaches a peak concentration around 2:00 A.M. When the eye is exposed to light, the production of melatonin is decreased or suppressed altogether. Body temperature, alertness, and mood are also intimately linked to the periodicity of the sleep-wake cycle. Body temperature is lowest in the early morning (4:00 A.M.), starts rising before one wakes, peaks in the early evening, and begins declining about 11:00 P.M. Alertness is best at the high point of the body temperature curve, and sleepiness is most intense at its lowest point. Naturally, we are slower physically and mentally during the early morning hours, and become more energetic and productive in the latter part of the morning, when our temperature rises.

Experts believe that in addition to the light-dark cycle, other time markers from the environment (clocks, mealtimes, work schedules), also called *Zeitgebers,* are extremely important in keeping our body's rhythms in a state of equilibrium. Imagine living in isolation from the outside world. You are free to eat, sleep, and do what you want when you feel like it, but you have no time cues, no radio or television, no newspapers, and no social contacts. Experiments conducted with volunteers living in specially designed apartments shielded from the outside world have shown that most people chose to live on a cycle of 25 to 26 hours instead of the 24-hour cycle we usually assume. When periods of isolation were prolonged for about 1 month, subjects functioned for much longer periods, sometimes awake for 20 hours and asleep for 10 hours, as the sleep-wake cycle became desynchronized with many of the body's other rhythms. Consequently, we can assume light and social time markers keep our biological clock in tune with the outside world.

ARE YOU A MORNING PERSON (LARK) OR A NIGHT PERSON (OWL)?

While body's rhythms are fairly consistent among most people, there are individual differences and preferences. Larks, or morning persons, are naturally early risers and tend to function best in the morning. They also get sleepy earlier in the evening and like to go to bed early. Night owls take longer to get going in the morning and enjoy sleeping late. Once they get started, they are harder to stop and tend to function best in the evening and even late at night. They adapt more easily to work-shift changes than do the morning-type persons, who do not tolerate schedule changes very well. Some studies suggest that larks are more quiet and introverted, whereas owls are more outgoing and energetic, although these traits do not apply universally by any means.

WHEN YOUR BIOLOGICAL CLOCK IS OUT OF SYNC WITH THE OUTSIDE WORLD

Several problems can arise when your body clock is no longer synchronized with the external world. In the remainder of this chapter, we describe some of those conditions and discuss the methods to correct them or to minimize their effect on your life.

Delayed Sleep Phase Syndrome

In delayed sleep phase syndrome, the major sleep period is delayed in relation to its desired timing. It is characterized by the person's intractable difficulty falling asleep until late in the night (e.g., 3:00 A.M.). Once the person does fall asleep, she or he usually has no difficulty staying asleep. When there is no required rising time, such as on weekends or during vacations, the problem is circumvented, because the sleep duration will be normal even if it is delayed. The obligation to arise at a conventional time in the morning to go to work, to school, or take care of the children becomes extremely difficult to meet, given the short duration of the sleep period. College students and people working shifts often develop this condition. Irregular sleep schedules or frequent switching of bedtimes and rising times tend to desynchronize the circadian rhythms. Recent research has linked this type of sleep-onset insomnia to a delay in the body temperature decline, which typically occurs around 11:00 P.M. Two treatment methods described later in this chapter, chronotherapy and light therapy, can be helpful when insomnia is due to a stubborn clock. Exposure to bright light in the early morning hours can help advance the timing of your bedtime and rising time. In addition, several of the procedures described in Chapter 6 can help alleviate the condition.

Advanced Sleep Phase Syndrome

Sometimes the body clock runs too fast rather than too slow, so sleep comes too soon and ends too early. This is the advanced sleep phase syndrome. The difficulty in staying awake in the evening (after 8:00 or 9:00 P.M.) is followed by early morning awakening (4:00 A.M.). Total sleep duration is not necessarily shortened, and people with this problem do not necessarily choose to go to bed early in the evening. They are simply unable to remain awake until their desired bedtime. More frequent in older adults, the condition is similar to the problem of early morning awakening that is often experienced in late life. In the latter case, however, a person may be wide awake at 4:00 A.M. even though bedtime was around 11:00 or even midnight. To distinguish between those two conditions, one should consider the actual duration of sleep instead of relying exclusively on the clock time at the final awakening. As for delayed phase problems, the behavior and schedule changes outlined in Chapter 6 can be helpful. Also, bright light exposure in the evening, not in the morning, can push back the body clock timing. This is discussed later in the chapter.

Jet Lag

Business or pleasure takes an increasing number of travelers across the time zones. For several days after arrival, most complain of jet lag: they feel sleepy when others are awake, they are hungry when restaurants are closed, and they are ready to do business or have fun when others are sleeping. Their internal clocks are out of sync with the new time zone. Imagine flying from New York on a typical red-eye (night) flight, leaving around 10:00 P.M., traveling for about six hours, and arriving in London around 10:00 the next morning, which would be 4:00 A.M. according to your home time. Needless to say, this might not be the most opportune time to enjoy a sightseeing tour or to negotiate an important contract with a foreign corporation.

The effects of jet lag are fatigue, lethargy, sleepiness, and a general malaise. There is also a sense of disorientation, and both concentration and judgment are disrupted. These effects, which last for several days, can be unpleasant and costly. If you travel across six to nine time zones for a typical trip from North America to Europe, and have only a week of vacation, you may find yourself struggling throughout your stay to enjoy your vacation. Likewise, if you are on a business trip, jet lag may impair your abilities to make the best decisions when working out an important deal.

Two important factors determine the severity of jet lag symptoms: the direction of the flight and the number of time zones crossed. Jet lag is specific to transmeridian flights, those headed east or west. Fatigue, sleepiness, and disorientation are also commonly experienced on flights bound north or south, although they are often produced by other factors, such as high altitude, alcohol, vibration, noise, turbulence, flight anxiety, and sleep loss and excitement occurring before departure. Unlike jet lag, these symptoms usually subside within 24 to 48 hours of arrival, especially with a good night's sleep. After traveling across time zones, you may need several days to synchronize your biological clock with the new destination clock time. Studies of air travelers indicate that after a westbound flight, the body clock needs about a day to adjust to the local time for each time zone (hour) crossed. Recovery time may even be longer after an eastbound flight.

One study found that air travelers took an average of 12 days to adjust completely following a trip from the West Coast to Europe.

Why does it take longer to adjust to an eastbound flight? The body's natural tendency to function on a slightly longer than 24-hour day makes it easier to lengthen than to shorten our days. When you travel west, your body clock is ahead of the local time. For example, on your first night after a flight from Washington to San Francisco, the local time may be 9:00 P.M., Pacific Time, but your body clock is set at midnight. To speed up adaptation, you have to keep yourself awake until the customary local bedtime; and it is easier to force wakefulness than to force sleep. On the other hand, on your return to the East Coast, your body clock may lag behind. When your home clock says it is bedtime—for example, 11:00 P.M. Eastern Time—your body clock is still set at 8:00 P.M. In this case, your obligations dictate a bedtime that is too early for your body, and you may find it very difficult if not impossible to force yourself to sleep.

How to Minimize Jet Lag

If you are planning to travel across three or more time zones you can take several measures to ease jet lag before you leave home or after arriving at your destination.

Start living on your destination time when you board the aircraft, or as soon as practically possible before departure. Set your wristwatch to the destination time; schedule your meals, activities, and sleep periods closer and closer to the destination time. For example, in anticipation of a westbound flight, go to bed and arise an hour later than usual. For an eastbound flight, go to bed and arise an hour earlier than usual. If you can do that for several days before departure day, you will already have a jump start on adjusting to jet lag once you arrive at your destination.

Upon arrival, adjust your sleep schedule to the local one. After a long journey across five or more time zones, you may feel exhausted and ready to hit the sack. A short nap, less than an hour long, is acceptable to help you get through the day. However, avoid a prolonged nap. Stay awake during the local wake period so that you'll sleep during the new nocturnal period.

Allow some time to recover. On transcontinental flights, do not schedule important business meetings on arrival. Instead, try to arrive a day or two early to give your mind and body time to overcome fatigue and disorientation and to recover from jet lag.

If your trip is to be a short one, 2 or 3 days, stay on your home time. Keep your watch set on home time and sleep according to your usual home schedule. Take advantage of your body's natural rhythms and try to schedule meetings based on the time when you function best at home. If your alertness, concentration, and mental skills are at peak around 11:00 A.M., and you are traveling to New York from the West Coast, take care of business around 2:00 P.M.

Be careful with alcohol. High altitude intensifies the effects of alcohol. Some researchers estimate that two or three cocktails consumed at 12,000 feet in the air have an effect equivalent to that of four or five drinks at sea level.

A hypnotic medication may be of some help. If you are on a red-eye flight and travel for several hours, a hypnotic drug may make it easier for you to sleep on the plane. Ask your doctor for a very short-acting sleeping pill, one that is rapidly eliminated from the body so that it will not interfere with your functioning the next day.

Careful exposure to light and dark can help adjust your sleep pattern to a new time zone. The timing of light and dark exposure is critical to obtaining the desired shift in your circadian rhythm. Below is an example of how to minimize jet lag for a nighttime eastbound flight in which you will be crossing six time zones, let's say from Boston to Paris. The goal is to advance your body clock as rapidly as possible to match the time in Europe.

From about 10:00 P.M., your original time, keep your surroundings as dark as possible. To minimize light exposure, you can use dark sunglasses or goggles. A cloth eye mask is ideal during sleep. If you are already at the airport awaiting your flight, put on your sunglasses even if people around may wonder what's wrong with you. Once you are in your seat, close the window shade, and keep it closed during the flight. Daylight will come much faster than you may expect because of the quick change in time. Use your eye mask when sleeping, because a small amount of light can get through closed eyes. On your arrival, around 9:00 or 10:00 A.M., put away the sunglasses and get outdoors for at least several hours. Exposure to daylight and a steady flow of activity will help you beat jet lag. You may be tired—you may dream of going to bed—but stay outside for daylight exposure and try to remain active through the day. If you have to be indoors, stay close to a window to get maximal exposure to daylight.

On the next night, go to bed between 9:00 and midnight, local time. Avoid staying up late. If you wake up during the night—which is a real possibility—stay in the dark. Any exposure to light after 10:00 P.M. local time will set you back in your efforts. Keep your surroundings dark until 8:00 A.M., and put on your sunglasses if you wake up before that time. On your second day, stay outdoors and active, especially during the first four hours of the day. The following night, go to bed before midnight and, again, avoid light exposure until the next morning. On the third day, rise at the desired time and stay on a regular schedule. By then, most of your jet lag symptoms should be gone.

Reverse these general guidelines when you travel west. In this case, the goal is to delay your body clock to match local time. Maximize daylight exposure in the evening and minimize it in the early part of the day. If you would like more information on this topic, consult an excellent book, *How to Beat Jet Lag,* written by four experts at the National Institute of Mental Health. It provides step-by-step instructions for lessening jet lag on flights anywhere around the globe.

Shift Work: Jet Lag Without Leaving Home

Between 20 to 25 percent of employees (27 percent of men and 16 percent of women) spend some hours on evening or night shifts. Nurses, police officers, doctors, pilots, truck drivers, factory workers, and many others often work in rotating shifts, on duty during the day for a set period of time (e.g., 1 week), then on an evening shift for a similar period, followed by a night shift. This kind of schedule is like working for a week in Tokyo, a week in San Francisco, and a week in Paris. It requires constant resetting of the biological clock, and has inevitable effects on one's health and well-being. Many of the symptoms associated with shift work are similar to those of jet lag, except that they are more pervasive—and the person doesn't get to travel anywhere.

Shift workers have more difficulty sleeping than people on a normal daytime working schedule. On average, night workers sleep 5 to 7 hours per week less than day workers; their daytime sleep is lighter and more frequently interrupted. Night workers often have difficulty falling asleep during the day and staying awake at night. As a result, they may consume more sedatives and more stimulants. Excessive caffeine intake, combined with irregular meal schedules, leads to frequent gastrointestinal problems. In addition, the sleeping time of a shift worker is not as protected as that of other employees. Telephones, doorbells, noises from the children and the street, and many other disturbances occur during the daytime and diminish at night. Shift workers need to expend considerable extra effort to protect their sleep time. Although many of them attempt to catch up on sleep during their days off, they function in a constant state of sleep deprivation, which naturally affects mood, quality of life, alertness, and performance.

Problems like irritability, fatigue, and difficulty concentrating are extremely common among shift workers, as is the strain on marital and family relations. Someone on the graveyard shift has less time to spend with a spouse and with children, to socialize, or even to run errands. Our society is organized to suit the conventional working day, and it may be difficult for a shift worker to socialize with friends who are locked into a different timetable, or to take part in community activities. Social isolation can be a real problem.

Shift work can also be a serious public hazard. About 20 percent of employees working the evening shift, and 53 percent of those working the night shift, acknowledge dozing off on the job. Dr. Torbjorn Akerstedt of Sweden monitored brain-wave activity of locomotive engineers during night trips. He found that, although few of the engineers admitted falling asleep, several did drift in and out of micro-sleep episodes, lasting a few seconds, without even being aware of it. Numerous road, rail, air, and maritime accidents have been linked to human error caused by sleepiness on the job at night. The *Exxon Valdez* grounding occurred around midnight; the near disaster at the Three Mile Island nuclear power plant took place at 4:00 A.M. The Chernobyl nuclear disaster in Ukraine also took place at night.

Coping with Shift Work

Some people prefer working evening or night shifts, but the majority do so because of job requirements. Some people also adjust more easily than others. The night owls tend to be more awake at night and adapt more easily than the larks. Younger people also adjust better. Many of those who have been on a rotating schedule for most of their adult lives find it harder to tolerate when they reach their forties or fifties. Working a straight evening or night shift is easier than rotating schedules, so whether it is by choice or by obligation, a constantly changing schedule is likely to affect the quality of your sleep and of your life more than a regular daytime shift. The following recommendations can help you cope with shift work and minimize its negative consequences.

Rotate shifts from days to evenings to nights. Shifts that rotate clockwise from days to evenings to nights are easier to adapt to than shifts that rotate in a counterclockwise direction. This rotation takes advantage of our natural tendency to function on days that are slightly longer than 24 hours, and on the fact that it is easier to lengthen our days than to shorten them.

Rotate shifts every 2 or 3 days, or remain on the same shift for a period of 2 to 3 weeks. Conventional shifts often rotate every week, placing a person's body clock in chronic need of readjustment. A more frequently rotating schedule (2 to 3 days) keeps the body on a diurnal cycle, whereas one that rotates only every 2 or 3 weeks gives the body enough time to adapt fully to a new circadian rhythm.

If you are on a straight night or evening shift, maintain the same schedule on your days off. If you return to a daytime schedule on your days off, you will need a new adjustment whenever you go back to work. Practically, it is difficult for those who have a family and a social life to adhere to such a regimen.

If you are on rotating shifts, begin adjusting your sleep schedule before you move to the new shift. For example, a day or two before you switch from the evening to the night shift, schedule your sleep period 1 or 2 hours later than usual. When you start the night shift, your body clock will already have begun its adjustment, easing the transition.

Similarly, before you go from a night to a day shift, schedule your sleep period 1 or 2 hours later than usual. This will ease the return to a normal nighttime sleep schedule.

Protect your sleep time. There are many disruptions that interfere with the quality of daytime sleep. Make sure you unplug the telephone, post a DO NOT DISTURB sign on your door, and schedule your sleep period when everyone else in the house is gone for the day. Tell your relatives or friends not to visit on those days. Use ear plugs or "white noise" to minimize noise.

Keep your bedroom environment completely dark. Even a tiny amount of daylight coming through the windows may interfere with your sleep and prevent your body clock from adjusting to its new schedule. Use an eye mask and dark curtains or shades for the bedroom windows.

Maintain good sleep hygiene. Keep a regular sleep schedule, avoid stimulants before bedtime, and do not try to force sleep. Shift workers are at greater risk of insomnia than those working on a regular daytime schedule, so it is twice as important for them to follow all the behavioral principles outlined in previous chapters. Ideally, it is best to get your sleep in one stretch; if that doesn't work, schedule two separate sleep episodes, one in the morning and one in the late afternoon or the early part of the evening. Although napping is generally not recommended for insomnia, a short nap may help shift workers compensate for shorter sleep episodes during the day and ensure their adequate alertness throughout the night. The value of sleeping pills to improve daytime sleep is controversial among experts. An occasional hypnotic may help, but there is little evidence that improved sleep during the day enhances alertness or performance at night.

OTHER METHODS TO RESET YOUR BODY'S RHYTHMS
Chronotherapy

Chronotherapy consists of moving ahead your bedtime by 3 hours every day. For example, if your usual bedtime is 11:00 P.M., move it the first night to 2:00 A.M., the second one to 5:00 A.M., the third one to 8:00 A.M., and so on until you have gone around the clock to the desired bedtime. As bedtime moves from late night to early morning hours, afternoon, and back to evening, the total sleep period time remains constant at eight hours. The sleep period is gradually advanced from 11:00 P.M. to 7:00 A.M., 2:00 A.M. to 10:00 A.M., 5:00 A.M. to 1:00 P.M. It may take between 1 and 2 weeks to go around the clock.

This treatment is designed for those insomnia sufferers with a stubborn internal clock, one that is delayed relative to the desired sleep schedule. Chronotherapy does require cooperation from family members and may even call for your taking time off from work. Sometimes the same results can be achieved by enforcing a strict rising time in the morning, along with implementing the other procedures outlined in Chapter 6.

Light Therapy

Light therapy is a fairly new treatment for some forms of insomnia associated with irregularities of the body clock. As previously discussed, the light-dark cycle has a major influence on the timing of the sleep-wake cycle and many other biological functions. Darkness activates secretion of the hormone melatonin, whereas light suppresses its production. Body temperature is also closely tied to sleep and alertness; it is lowest when sleepiness is most intense (around 4:00 A.M.) and reaches a peak when alertness is greatest (late morning). Exposure to bright light can shift your body's rhythms forward or backward and synchronize your internal clock with the desired schedule.

The direction and amount of the shift depends in large part on two factors: the timing and the intensity of light exposure. Bright light exposure in the evening delays your circadian rhythms, keeping you alert and making you want to go to bed later. Bright light exposure in the morning hours has the opposite effect; it advances your circadian rhythms, making you sleepy earlier in the evening. The intensity of the light is also important in determining the magnitude of the effect. Exposure to natural sunlight can be very helpful in minimizing the impact of jet lag. Typically, however, a very bright light (about 2,500 lux, which is about 5 times as bright as a well-lit office) is necessary to maximize the desired shift in circadian rhythms. Bright light boxes are sold by several companies. If you intend to use one, get advice from a sleep expert to determine the most effective intensity, timing, and duration of light exposure for your type of insomnia. You should never stare directly at the light. Also, remember that if it is improperly used, bright light exposure may have a counterproductive effect on your sleep-wake pattern.

Preliminary studies have shown that light therapy, also called phototherapy, is a promising approach for treating a variety of sleep disorders. Studies conducted by Dr. Charles Czeisler and his collaborators at Harvard University have shown that it can help night-shift workers get better sleep during the day and remain more alert at night. Other studies have shown that it can also be helpful for some forms of insomnia. Exposure to bright light in the early morning hours can help those who suffer from delayed sleep phase syndrome by advancing the time at which they feel sleepy. For those who suffer from the advanced sleep phase syndrome, and are sleepy too early in the evening and awake too early in the morning, evening light exposure can push back the body's rhythm. This is a potentially useful approach for correcting early morning awakenings, so commonly experienced by older people. Some preliminary work with air travelers and pilots suggest that bright light exposure before departure or on arrival at the destination can speed up the synchronization with the local time and decrease the intensity and duration of jet lag symptoms. Light therapy has also been helpful in treating those with seasonal affective disorder, a form of depression associated with reduced light exposure. In the winter, when the days are shorter, and in some of the northern countries, where daylight is completely absent for several days, seasonal depression and sleep-wake problems are common.

Melatonin

Melatonin, a hormone secreted by the pineal gland at night, is at its highest concentration around 2:00 A.M. Exposure to light suppresses its production. Researchers speculate that administration of a synthetic melatonin product at bedtime may be the closest thing to taking a natural sleeping pill. Can melatonin alleviate jet lag? Some experts believe that administration of melatonin at the right time will fool the body and speed up resynchronization of its circadian rhythms following rapid time zone changes. Although this is a promising avenue for further research, it is too early to say whether the natural hormone is truly effective.

11

The Hazards
of Sleeping Pills

Drug therapy is by far the most frequently used method for treating insomnia. Estimates from large surveys indicate that about 7 percent of the population use a prescribed or over-the-counter sleep medication during the course of a year. A Gallup survey conducted in 1991 also showed that 21 percent of people who suffer from insomnia had taken a prescribed sleeping pill at some time in the past and 28 percent had used alcohol as a sleep aid. Sleeping pills are used in greater proportion by women, older adults, and by people with higher stress levels and more medical problems. In this chapter we review the different types of medications used as sleep aids, show how they affect your sleep, explain their adverse effects and limitations, and indicate when they can help or should be avoided. For those who may have become dependent on sleeping pills, a step-by-step withdrawal program is outlined to help you kick the sleeping pill habit.

Types of Sleep Medications

There is a wide variety of medications prescribed for sleep (see Table 11.1). Half a dozen drugs are approved by the Food and Drug Administration to be marketed specifically as sleeping pills, also known as hypnotics. Five of them belong to a class of medications known as the benzodiazepines: ProSom, Dalmane, Doral, Restoril, and Halcion. Ambien is the most recently FDA-approved hypnotic; it belongs to a different class of chemical. There are also the drugs known as benzodiazepine-anxiolytics, which are prescribed for insomnia when anxiety is part of the sleep problem. Some of the most widely prescribed are Ativan, Xanax, and Valium. Even some antidepressant drugs are prescribed as sleeping aids. A popular antidepressant such as Prozac has an energizing effect and may actually cause insomnia, whereas others (e.g., Elavil, Sinequan) produce drowsiness as a side effect. To take advantage of that side effect, some physicians prescribe those drugs for treating insomnia, but in much smaller doses than would be used for depression. The risk of addiction to an antidepressant is much smaller than that with traditional sleeping pills, though they also have more side effects. In addition, these drugs, well studied for treating depression, are usually not recommended for treating nondepressed insomniacs.

Some older drugs, popular in the 1960s and 1970s, are rarely prescribed today because of their risks of habituation, toxic effects, and interactions with other drugs. These include meprobamate, chloral hydrate, glutethimide, and a general class of drug known as the barbiturates (e.g., Seconal, Nembutal). Although some elderly persons may still be using those medications, much safer drugs are available today.

A number of over-the-counter (OTC) medications can be obtained without a physician's prescription: Sominex, Unisom, Sleep-Eze, Nytol. OTC sleep aids are probably much more widely used than prescribed hypnotics. The active ingredient in most of them is an antihistamine, diphenhydramine, similar to what is contained in cold and allergy medicines like Benadryl. Because drowsiness is a fairly common side effect of most antihistamines, drug companies have capitalized on this to market the drugs as sleep-promoting agents. Despite millions of dollars spent in advertising, there is essentially no scientific evidence that these agents are effective for insomnia. They may produce drowsiness but they are rarely powerful enough to put an anxious person to sleep. Sometimes an antihistamine can have the opposite effect and make you more uptight, wired, and sleepless. Although some people claim that such an aid, or even two aspirins at bedtime,

Table 11.1. MEDICATIONS COMMONLY PRESCRIBED FOR INSOMNIA

Chemical or Generic Name	Commercial or Trade Name	Usual Nightly Dosage Range (mg)
Hypnotics		
Estazolam*	ProSom	1–2
Flurazepam*	Dalmane	7.5–30
Flunitrazepam+	Rohypnol	1–4
Quazepam*	Doral	7.5–30
Temazepam*	Restoril	7.5–30
Triazolam* ■	Halcion	0.125–0.25
Nitrazepam+	Mogadon	5–10
Zolpidem*	Ambien	5–10
Zopiclone+	Imovan	3.75–7.5
Anxiolytics		
Alprazolam	Xanax	0.25–2
Chlordiazepoxide	Librium	10–30
Clonazepam	Klonopin	0.5–2
Clorazepate	Tranxene	3.75–15
Diazepam	Valium	5–10
Lorazepam	Ativan	0.5–3
Oxazepam	Serax	10–30
Prazepam	Centrax	5–30
Anti-Depressants		
Amitriptyline	Elavil	10–50
Doxepin	Sinequan or Adapin	10–50
Trazodone	Desyrel	25–100
Trimipramine	Surmontil	10–50

* These drugs are specifically approved by the Food and Drug Administration as hypnotic medications in the United States.

+ These drugs are available in Canada and some European countries but not in the United States.

■ Triazolam has been banned in several European countries.

help them to sleep, the efficacy of these self-remedies is doubtful. One has to remember that the placebo effect, or what one believes will happen after he takes a drug, can be quite powerful.

A synthetic melatonin is available in most health food stores and is marketed as a natural sleeping pill. However, it is not regulated by the FDA and is sold in much larger doses than what is produced by the pineal gland. Although some early research suggests that it may be useful, it is much too early to say whether it is of clinical benefit to those who have severe sleep difficulties.

Alcohol, we saw earlier in the book, is a depressant of the central nervous system. Although it may help a tense person get to sleep faster, it is not recommended as a sleeping aid, because its overall effect is of more fitful sleep. Once the body metabolizes the alcohol, there is a sort of mini-withdrawal syndrome that causes you to wake up earlier in the morning, sometimes with a hangover. Alcohol delays REM sleep in the early morning hours, and occasionally people wake up with unpleasant dreams, even nightmares.

How Drugs Affect Your Sleep

Most prescribed hypnotic medications can help you sleep better in the *short-term*. As a general rule, they shorten the time it takes to fall asleep, reduce the number and duration of awakenings, and, as a result, increase total sleep time. The effects vary with the medicines, depending on their chemical compositions. For example, drugs like Ambien and Halcion are more quickly absorbed in the bloodstream and have a faster onset, so they are better suited for difficulties in falling asleep. Others, like Restoril, take a little longer to be absorbed and their effects are delayed; still others, like Dalmane and Doral, have a quick and prolonged effect throughout the night. These are more appropriate for people who have trouble staying asleep.

Some Limitations of Sleeping Pills

Although most prescribed sleep medicines are effective in the short term, they have several shortcomings. Most important, all sleeping pills lose their efficacy when used on a nightly basis. When a hypnotic drug is used every night, the brain and body become habituated to the chemicals and develop what is called drug tolerance. When this happens, the dosage needs to be increased if the drug is to continue producing the desired effect. Although the time required to develop tolerance varies among individuals, whenever the highest safe dosage is reached, you are trapped in a dead-end situation. We will discuss later in this chapter how you can get out of the trap. For now, let's just say that for this reason, among others, all sleeping pills are designed for short-term usage. Soon or later, they all stop working. And additional problems are likely to arise, either during the course of drug therapy or after its discontinuation. Among them are alteration of sleep stages, daytime carry-over effects, rebound insomnia, and dependence.

All hypnotic drugs alter the architecture of sleep, that is, the proportion of time spent in the various sleep stages. Although the continuity and duration of sleep are improved, its quality is often diminished. For example, almost all hypnotics decrease stage 1 (light sleep) and increase stage 2 sleep. At the same time, however, they decrease the amount of time spent in stages 3–4 sleep, the deepest and most restorative sleep. Some drugs may also diminish REM or dream sleep, although this depends on dosage and can vary among medications. The reduction of REM sleep is more pronounced with older hypnotic drugs, such as the barbiturates, and with antidepressants. The exact significance of a reduction of REM sleep is not clear, but when these drugs are discontinued there is often an increase in the amount of REM sleep, which can be experienced as unpleasant dreams or nightmares.

Perhaps one of the most intriguing aspects of hypnotic medications is that their objective effects on sleep as measured by brain-wave activity do not necessarily correspond to the subjective perception of sleep quality. The following vignette illustrates the point.

Peter had used sleeping pills for the last 10 years, switching from Dalmane to Ativan and to Halcion. When he came for his overnight test in our sleep clinic, he had forgotten his pills, and panicked. He was very concerned that he might never sleep, and he called his wife to bring his Halcion. Since we were interested in getting a sample of his typical sleep patterns, this was fine with us. The next morning, after the technician had scored the more than thousand-page record, it looked as if Peter had slept for about 6 hours out of 8 spent in bed. Although he went to sleep within 15 minutes, his record showed that he spent an hour and a half awake during the night. When I asked Peter how he had slept in the clinic, he claimed, to my surprise, that he was asleep for most of the night, perhaps waking up once or twice but not for more than 10 to 15 minutes.

Scientists are finding that sleeping pills, especially the benzodiaze-pines, produce amnesia and alter sleep perception. They tend to impair the memory of events that occur after the medication is taken. For most insomniacs, this means that, even though sleep may remain disrupted when a hypnotic medication is used, there is little recall of those noc-turnal awakenings in the morning. The sleeping pill may work by clouding consciousness and impairing the memory of wakefulness. Pe-ter remembered only vaguely that he had been awake that night, but certainly not for an hour and a half. This phenomenon may explain why some people continue using sleep medication for years, despite objective evidence that it is no longer working.

What Are the Side Effects?

Hypnotic drugs can produce several adverse effects the next day: "drug hangover," drowsiness or anxiety, and impairment of perfor-mance. The nature and severity of these reactions vary with the type and amount of drug. For example, long-acting drugs, such as Dalmane, take longer to be metabolized and remain present in the system for a good part of the following day. These drugs are more likely to leave you with a feeling of being "hung over" the next morning; residual sleepiness may even carry through the day and interfere with your ability to drive your car or perform otherwise routine activities. Elderly people take longer to metabolize drugs, and those who use long-acting drugs are at greater risk of falls and hip fractures than those who use short-acting ones or no medication at all. Short-acting drugs are more rapidly eliminated, but they may produce anxiety or early morning awakening.

Although many people use a hypnotic medication to ensure that they'll function adequately the next day, there is little scientific evidence to support this assumption. Rather than improving waking functions, some hypnotics may adversely affect memory and concentration. Surprisingly, such an impairment is often mistakenly attributed to disturbed sleep, when in fact it may represent the carry-over effect of the sleeping pill. The initial benefits of a sleep medication must be weighed against its residual effects.

Another shortcoming of hypnotic medications is that they can have undesired interactions with other drugs you are using for medical problems. Always tell your doctor every medicine you are taking. Never mix alcohol with sleeping pills, as this can be a lethal combination.

A common problem that arises when a person attempts to stop using a hypnotic drug is rebound insomnia, an intense worsening of sleep difficulties. This phenomenon is particularly pronounced with short-acting drugs, because they are more quickly eliminated from the bloodstream. Rebound insomnia is often accompanied by severe anxiety, which reinforces the insomniac's belief that he cannot sleep without medication. It is therefore extremely powerful in prompting a person to resume medication and in promoting drug-dependency. We will return to this issue later.

When Can a Sleeping Pill Help?

The short-term use of a prescribed hypnotic medication may be appropriate in some situations. First, it may be helpful on a temporary basis if you develop acute and situational insomnia as a result of severe stressors in your life—the death of a loved one, impending surgery or hospitalization, separation, or divorce. Second, short-term use may be helpful for insomnia caused by jet lag or by some medical conditions. Third, if you have chronic sleep difficulties, occasional use of a hypnotic may break the vicious cycle of insomnia and performance anxiety. This approach, however, should be viewed as an adjunct to the main therapeutic methods, which focus on behavioral and attitudinal changes. Finally, people who have completed the nondrug treatment program described in this book sometimes feel that simply having sleeping aids available is helpful. It provides them with a sense of security and reduces their fear of becoming sleepless again. Under any circumstances, medications should be used only for a short period, usually no more than a few nights or, at most, a few weeks.

When Should They Be Avoided?

Sleeping pills should never be mixed with alcohol; both substances are depressants of the nervous system, and their combined effects can be very dangerous. Hypnotic drugs, like many other drugs, should not be used by pregnant women, because the chemicals cross the placenta and may affect the development of the unborn baby. They should not be used if you may unexpectedly be called on duty in the middle of the night. If you try to come out of a drug-induced sleep before the effect has worn off, your alertness, judgment, and performance may be impaired for some time. Do not use sleep medications if you have symptoms of sleep apnea, a sleep-related breathing problem; all hypnotic drugs slow down respiration and worsen the breathing problem. An occasional hypnotic may be helpful for someone who suffers from an anxiety disorder, but you should avoid it if the suspected diagnosis is depression. All hypnotics have as their main effect the slowing down of the central nervous system. In depressed persons, these drugs will only aggravate the symptoms. When insomnia is associated with a psychiatric disorder, it is best managed by treatment of the underlying condition with psychotherapy, drug therapy, or a combination of both.

Older people should be particularly cautious when using hypnotic drugs. Since they are more sensitive to these drugs than younger adults, their doses should be smaller. Also, they metabolize drugs more slowly than younger people and are especially at risk of the toxic effects of long-acting drugs, which may not have time to be completely eliminated when used every night. Hypnotic drugs can create confusion in the person getting up at night to go to the bathroom or arising the next morning. Older adults using sleeping pills, particularly long-acting ones, are at increased risk of falls and hip fractures. Residual effects such as daytime sleepiness and reduced alertness while driving are also more pronounced in the elderly. Because older adults generally use more drugs for other medical conditions, they are also at greater risk of untoward drug interactions.

In summary, occasional use of a hypnotic can be helpful in dealing with acute insomnia, but it generally loses effectiveness fairly quickly with nightly use. The initial benefits must be weighed against the day-time sequelae and the potential in causing dependency when used over a prolonged period.

How You Can Become Addicted to Sleeping Pills

Not everyone using a sleeping pill during a stressful period of life will become addicted to the drug; the danger lies in prolonged use. Drug-dependency rarely develops overnight; rather, it evolves gradually with use, tolerance, withdrawal, dependence (see Figure 11.1). Most people are typically introduced to hypnotics during periods of stress, during hospitalization, or when they can no longer cope with chronic insomnia.

Figure 11.1. The Cycle of Drug Dependency

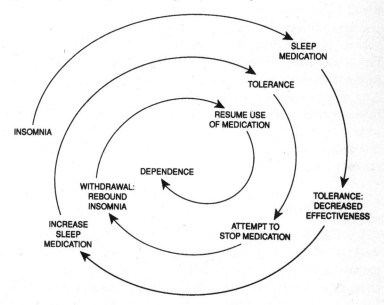

Prescriptions are sometimes renewed (over the phone) even though the insomnia may have subsided. With nightly use, your body habitu-ates and you develop tolerance; increased dosage is then required to achieve any hypnotic effects. When the maximum safe dosage has been reached, you are trapped in a dead-end situation. The sleeping pill may no longer work, yet any attempt to discontinue it is followed by greater sleep difficulties, sometimes worse than they were before. It is then that many people enter a cycle of catastrophic thinking and misinterpretation. Although rebound insomnia and withdrawal effects are usually temporary, these symptoms often lead to excessive concern that insomnia has returned for good and that the sleeping pill is needed. When the medication is resumed after several sleepless nights, of course it works at first. This only reinforces the belief that medication is indeed necessary and perpetuates the vicious cycle of drug-dependency.

Sleeping pills prescribed today are less addictive, in the physiological sense, than those used twenty or thirty years ago. However, drug-dependent insomnia is often more psychological than physical in nature, and some people may even become dependent on over-the-counter drugs. Conditioning plays an important role in the compulsive use of hypnotics. Insomnia and its sequelae are often seen as an aversive state. Because an occasional sleeping pill may eliminate this unpleasant state, the drug-taking behavior is reinforced. To maintain efficacy and prevent tolerance, sleeping pills are typically prescribed to be used only as needed ("prn"). This intermittent schedule is quite powerful in perpetuating a self-contained yet habitual pattern of use: you have insomnia, use medication, develop tolerance, try to stop the medication, experience rebound insomnia, and resume the drug. And you end up with two problems instead of one: insomnia and addiction to sleeping pills.

A Self-Guided Program to Quit the Sleeping Pill Habit

If you have been using sleeping pills regularly for more than a few weeks, it may be time to consider kicking the habit. No sleeping pill on the market today produces what is called natural sleep. You cannot buy sleep, even with the best drug in the world. Soon or later there will be a backlash. You are probably well aware of those facts, yet, like the majority of insomnia sufferers seeking help at our clinic, you may also feel trapped. In this section, you will learn effective strategies for quitting sleeping pills. Before you begin to wean yourself, talk to your prescribing doctor or your pharmacist about your plan. Ideally, you should discuss the proposed plan here with your physician and adapt it to the specific type of medication and dosage you are using.

1. Select a Target Date

Pick the date for beginning your withdrawal program and make this date known to your spouse, a close friend, or some relatives. This public commitment shores up your motivation to move forward and to obtain the needed social support. Select a time when your life is not too chaotic. If you are going through a separation or a change of jobs, it is not the right time to undertake this program. On the other hand, don't wait for everything to be perfect and orderly in your life. Once the program is under way, set the tentative date when you expect to be completely drug-free. The idea here is to keep the program limited in time.

2. Keep a Record of Your Progress

Keep a record of your medication intake—the type of sleep aid, dosage, and frequency of use. This information should already be available from your daily sleep diaries. Keep a weekly summary of your progress. Make a copy of the blank form (Table 11.3) that is like the example shown in Table 11.2. Set a weekly goal for reductions in dosage and number of medicated nights. Then, determine your confidence levels (on a scale of 0 to 100 percent) in achieving that goal. Set realistic and attainable goals, not excessively high ones, lest you shatter your self-confidence. If for any given week your confidence level is less than 75 percent, stay on the same schedule for another week in order to gain a greater sense of control and mastery.

3. Get Stable on Only One Hypnotic Drug

If you've been using more than one sleep medicine, the first step is to stick with only one. Chronic users of sleeping pills may at times alternate or, worse, combine two or three different medications. While switching drugs may sound like a good strategy to minimize your tolerance of any single one, it is not a good idea to mix sleeping pills. It may even be dangerous. If you have reached this point, the first step is to get stable on only one medication for at least a week, preferably longer.

Table 11.2. EXAMPLE OF MEDICATION WITHDRAWAL SCHEDULE

Week	Type/ Dosage (mg)	No. of Med. Nights	Total Weekly Amount (mg)	% Dosage Reduction	% Self-Confidence
Week 1	Ativan/ 2 mg	7	14 mg	—	—
Week 2	Ativan/1.5	7	10.5	25%	80%
Week 3	Ativan/1	7	7	50%	65%
Week 4	Ativan/0.5	7	3.5	75%	75%
Week 5	Ativan/0.5	5	2.5	82%	80%
Week 6	Ativan/0.5	3	1.5	89%	75%
Week 7	Ativan/0.5	2	1	93%	60%
Week 8	Ativan/0.5	1	0.5	96%	80%
Week 9	No drug	0	0	100%	75%

4. Reduce Your Medication Gradually, Never Quit Cold Turkey

If you've been using hypnotic medication nightly for more than a few nights, you should reduce the amount of medication in a gradual fashion to minimize withdrawal symptoms. Never stop at once. If you do, those withdrawal symptoms will be more severe, even dangerous, and the chances are that you will simply go back on the medication.

Decrease your medication by about 25 percent of its original dose. For example, if you are taking 2 mg of Ativan, the first cut would be down to 1.5 mg. Stay on this amount for an entire week, even if after a few nights you feel confident in decreasing it further. Avoid going back up to the original dosage, even if you experience some worsening of sleep difficulties.

Table 11.3. PERSONAL RECORD OF SLEEP
MEDICATION WITHDRAWAL SCHEDULE

Week	Type/ Dosage (mg)	No. of Med. Nights	Total Weekly Amount (mg)	% Dosage Reduction	% Self- Confidence
Week 1					
Week 2					
Week 3					
Week 4					
Week 5					
Week 6					
Week 7					
Week 8					
Week 9					
Week 10					

Keep reducing your drug by 25 percent of the original dose until you have reached the lowest available dose. In our example, this means your next step is to decrease to 1 mg for a week and to 0.5 mg for the next one. At that stage, you have reached the lowest available dosage of Ativan. If you do not feel confident yet in moving to the next step, you may still be able to cut your pill in half for an additional week. Be careful, however, not to become so obsessed that you keep cutting and cutting your pill until there is barely anything left. This is quite common among chronic users of sleeping pills. Soon or later you have to let go of it and move on.

5. Introduce Drug Holidays

Once you have reached the lowest available dosage, it is time to introduce "drug holidays." Pick two nights during the upcoming week when you will not use any sleeping pill. Medication is allowed only on the remaining five nights, which you will also select ahead of time. Although you may have some apprehension about this important step, you can minimize the impact of drug discontinuation by selecting nights when your agenda for the next day is not too busy or demanding. For most people, it is easier to begin skipping the medication on the weekend. There is usually less pressure and work obligation, and the apprehension of daytime impairment is diminished. After about a week of medication-free nights on the weekend, take the ''drug holidays'' on week nights. Follow a similar strategy, that is, first select a night preceding a less demanding day.

6. Use Sleep Medication as Scheduled, Not as Needed

As you implement this last step, it is essential that you determine ahead of time which nights you will take your medication and which will be drug free. Do not change your plan along the way. On selected drug-free nights, do not take your medication even if you are having a miserable night. Remember, some sleepless nights are to be expected in the short run, and they are only temporary. Conversely, on the nights you have chosen to take medication, take your pill at a fixed time (e.g., 30 minutes before bedtime) whether or not you believe you need it. As we said before, one reason you may have become dependent on sleeping pills is that the pill-taking behavior is reinforced by the relief of a very unpleasant state (sleeplessness). The strategy here is to eliminate or weaken the association between sleeplessness and drug-taking.

Once you are down to only one or two medicated nights per week, the final step is simply to go without the medication. Perhaps once you've reached this level you may be tempted to continue it. Don't get stuck there. Remember that this is probably how you became dependent on sleeping pills in the first place.

Congratulations! Now you are drug free. You certainly have good reason to be proud of yourself, because this is not an easy task. Make sure to reward yourself and to let other people know what you have accomplished.

7. Coping with Lapses

While you are weaning yourself from sleeping pills, you *may* have lapses along the way, or even after you have reached a drug-free state. If this happens, try to limit the damage. Having a lapse under difficult circumstances doesn't mean you have to go back on the pill every night. Do not get discouraged, and do not punish yourself with negative statements such as ''It's hopeless. I'm a loser.'' Instead, use positive statements to boost your self-confidence: ''I can do this. I will succeed at this.'' An important factor in successful change is the expectation of a positive outcome. Do not expect too much at once. Replacing old habits with new ones takes time. After all, if you've been using sleeping pills for months or years, it's to be expected that it will take time to stop.

A useful strategy to prevent lapses is to identify, ahead of time, high-risk situations, those you have had a difficult time with in the past, like preparing to leave on a trip or getting ready for an important meeting. Rather than using a sleeping pill on such a night, you should rely on your newly learned skills, such as restricting your time in bed and making sure you go to bed only when you're very sleepy.

WHAT YOU CAN EXPECT FROM THE PROGRAM

This gradual program has been found effective with many insomnia sufferers who were dependent on sleeping pills. It is not an easy task, but if you carefully follow the outlined program, there is every reason to believe you will be successful. If you are unsuccessful in getting off medication with this program, talk to your doctor or a professional therapist, who can assist you along the way. The time required to discontinue medication completely depends on the type of medication, its dosage, and the frequency and duration of its use. As a rule, a period of between 6 and 10 weeks is sufficient for most people to discontinue their medications. Even if you are eager to sleep without drugs, don't try to implement this program too quickly.

There are a number of withdrawal effects that you may experience as you discontinue sleeping pills; among them are a worsening of sleep difficulties, anxiety, irritability, fatigue, and heightened sensory perception. Be prepared for these adverse symptoms as the medication is discontinued. Keep in mind, however, that not everyone experiences the symptoms, and even if you do, they are minimized when you follow a gradual withdrawal schedule. All symptoms are temporary in nature. If you experience those effects, do not become anxious or depressed. It does not necessarily mean that your insomnia has returned. You may suffer for a little while, but things will surely get better.

When should you implement the program? The best time is after you have learned the methods for dealing with insomnia described in the previous chapters. These strategies should come in very handy, especially if you experience a worsening of sleep difficulties as you reduce your sleep medication. Occasionally, hypnotic discontinuation can completely cure a sleep problem after a person has gone through the expected withdrawal symptoms. More typically, you will experience sleep difficulties for some time after coming off the medication. That's when the coping strategies previously learned will help you deal with temporary setbacks.

Drug therapy alone is rarely effective in treating chronic insomnia. Clinical studies comparing psychological and drug therapies indicate that the latter may produce quicker results, whereas nondrug therapy may take a little longer but produces a more permanent improvement of sleep patterns. Nonetheless, a great deal of effort and money are being spent to develop the ideal drug for producing natural sleep. This perfect sleeping pill is not in sight, and even if it became available one day, no sleeping pill would cure insomnia, because pills do not address the underlying reason that sleep won't come; it only masks the problem and undermines the development of appropriate self-management skills. From a psychological perspective, sleep medication is likely to reinforce the perception that one is a victim of insomnia.

12

Other Sleep Disorders

Sleep disorders fall into four broad categories: (1) insomnia, difficulty sleeping at night; (2) hypersomnia, trouble staying awake during the day; (3) parasomnia, unusual or abnormal behavior during sleep; and (4) circadian rhythm disorders, problems in sleeping when desired and in staying awake when necessary, caused by such factors as jet lag or shift work. The main focus of this book has been on the various forms of insomnia, and circadian rhythm disorders were discussed in Chapter 10. In this chapter we describe other sleep disorders associated with excessive daytime sleepiness or with unusual behavior during sleep. It is important to note that any of those conditions can cause difficulty in sleeping at night, trouble staying awake during the day, or both. At times, you may be totally unaware of concealed symptoms until something abnormal is noted by a bedfellow or an overnight sleep study is conducted. Some of the disorders may be simple annoyances, others may diminish the quality of your life, and still others may be life-threatening.

SLEEP APNEA

Sleep apnea is a breathing disorder in which respiration, normal during wakefulness, is impaired during sleep. A person with sleep apnea stops breathing repeatedly during the night for periods of more than 10 seconds, sometimes up to a minute. The typical sequence of events involves complete or partial cessation of breathing, followed by a brief awakening, the resumption of breathing, accompanied by loud snorting and gasping sounds, and the return to sleep. Most of us experience a few lapses in breathing, especially as we are falling asleep at the beginning of the night. In severe cases, the cycle may repeat itself up to 200 or 300 times a night without the person being aware of it. The result is that, despite having spent eight hours in bed, apparently asleep, a person suffering from sleep apnea will wake up in the morning feeling dead tired and will have to struggle to stay awake through the day.

Sleep apnea is caused primarily by fat tissue in the back of the throat; as the person falls asleep the fat and muscles relax too much and block the airway. The main symptoms of apnea are loud snoring, pauses in breathing during sleep, which is typically witnessed by a bedfellow, restless sleep, and excessive daytime sleepiness. Occasionally, prolonged respiratory disturbances may lead the person to wake up gasping for air and experiencing an attack of panic followed by trouble returning to sleep. Most persons who suffer from apnea are unaware of the nocturnal symptoms, and their only subjective complaint is of the difficulty in staying awake during the day. Sleep apnea is particularly prevalent in obese middle-aged males and those with large necks; after menopause, women are also at risk.

Sleep apnea can have serious consequences on your health and mental ability and on public safety. Chronically poor-quality sleep inevitably leads to excessive daytime somnolence and the increased risk of falling asleep at the wheel or at other inappropriate times or places. Each time a person stops breathing, he or she has a decrease in the oxygen carried by the blood to the brain and other vital organs. Sleep apnea can produce hypertension and worsen most cardiovascular diseases. It may also produce deficits in memory and concentration and turn an otherwise happy and pleasant person into a depressed and very irritable one.

The most effective treatment option for sleep apnea is continuous positive airway pressure (CPAP). CPAP can be ensured by a small air compressor, connected by a plastic tube to a mask worn over your nose at night. The machine forces air through the nasal passages, keeping the airway open while you sleep. The CPAP machine is prescribed by a sleep specialist or a regular doctor once the diagnosis of sleep apnea has been made through an overnight sleep evaluation. There are several models available, sold by home health-care companies. You can rent the device for about $100 per month or buy it for about $1,000. Most insurance companies cover the cost of the device. Several other preventive or corrective measures can help in mild cases of sleep apnea. For example, avoid the bedtime use of alcohol or sleeping pills, which are two central nervous system depressants that slow down respiration. Avoid sleeping on your back, which worsens snoring and lapses in breathing. Because obesity is a risk factor for sleep apnea, weight loss can diminish the severity of the problem, although it is rarely sufficient in severe cases. Several forms of surgery are also available, ranging from the removal of tonsils and adenoids, laser-assisted burning of excess tissue at the back of the throat, repositioning the jaws to enlarge the airway; in life-threatening cases, a tracheostomy can be performed. Sleep apnea is the most frequently evaluated and treated condition in sleep disorders centers. When it is properly treated, patients are amazed at the amount of energy and vitality they can enjoy during the day.

SNORING IS NO LAUGHING MATTER

About 20 percent of the population snores habitually. Men tend to snore more than women, and the incidence increases as the person grows older. The noise we hear is caused by a vibration of the soft tissue (uvula and soft palate) against the back of the throat. Snoring is made worse by obesity, the use of alcohol and sedatives around bedtime, and sleeping in the supine position (lying on the back). Most of us have been kept awake or have made jokes about snorers. Sleeping with a partner who snores like a chain saw is no laughing matter, though; it can put a tremendous strain on a relationship, driving you crazy or at the very least into a separate room. Snoring diminishes the quality of sleep, both for the snorer and the bedfellow.

Is snoring just an annoying noise? Snoring in itself is not a sleep disorder, and mild snoring is not necessarily harmful, even though it can be very irritating to a captive audience. But loud snoring can, as we have just seen above, be a symptom of a more serious medical condition, sleep apnea.

What can be done to restore the sound of silence? For mild snoring, simple changes in body position can alleviate the problem. An anti-snore pillow, which keeps the neck straight, can help. Sewing a tennis ball into the back of a pajama top can discourage a person from sleeping on his or her back. New laser-assisted surgery is also available, although its efficacy is not yet well established. Anyone with chronic loud snoring, especially if it is punctuated by intermittent lapses in breathing lasting more than 10 seconds, should seek an evaluation from a sleep disorders specialist, as this may indicate sleep apnea.

RESTLESS LEGS SYNDROME

Restless legs syndrome (RLS) is characterized by an extremely uncomfortable sensation in the calves and by an irresistible urge to move the legs. Typically occurring between the knees and ankles, the discomfort may also involve the thighs, feet, knees, and even the arms. One of my recent patients with RLS described his condition in the following way: "It feels as if worms are crawling or creeping beneath the skin in my legs; every time I sit down or try to rest, I just can't keep my legs still. I need to move around all the time; it drives me crazy." The condition is worse when the legs are still, while the person is sitting watching television or is riding in or driving a car. It also worsens during the evening and particularly at bedtime. It can considerably delay sleep onset and may be the primary cause of insomnia. Walking or stretching of the legs can temporarily alleviate the unpleasant sensation. Many victims find themselves pacing the floor or exercising for hours before they finally doze off from pure exhaustion. RLS is not a condition recognized by most physicians; it must be differentiated from a general bodily restlessness seen in anxious individuals.

The causes of RLS are still not completely known. It is associated with iron deficiency and anemia, and is more frequent in pregnant women and in older people. Medical conditions accompanied by poor blood circulation, such as diabetes and renal diseases, are often associated with RLS. Most people who suffer from it also have a related condition known as periodic limb movements.

PERIODIC LIMB MOVEMENTS (PLM)

PLM, also called nocturnal myoclonus, is a series of brief and repetitive movements of the legs and arms. Unlike RLS, which is experienced during wakefulness, PLM occurs almost exclusively during sleep. More frequent in the first third of the night, these muscle contractions or jerks can occur several hundred times a night and are typically associated with awakenings lasting only a few seconds. Although in severe cases a person may wake up with leg cramps, typically the sleeper is unaware of the movements and has no memory of the wakenings. Yet sleep is interrupted and of poor quality, and the consequence is daytime sleepiness. This condition must be distinguished from the "hypnic jerk" or "sleep start," occurring at sleep onset or from periodic limb twitches occurring during REM sleep; both of these phenomena are entirely normal.

As with RLS, the prevalence of PLM increases significantly with age. Its causes are also unclear. It may be hereditary. It is frequently associated with deficiency of vitamin E, iron, or calcium, and with pain-related conditions, kidney disease, and other medical conditions causing poor blood circulation, such as diabetes. The subjective complaints associated with PLM are either difficulty maintaining sleep or excessive daytime sleepiness. At times, a person may be totally asymptomatic.

Treatment of PLM is not always required, as some people can sleep well through these limb movements and have no excessive daytime somnolence. For more severe cases, treatment for RLS and PLM is primarily medicinal. Three classes of drugs are prescribed for those conditions, including L-dopa (Sinemet), clonazepam (Klonopin), and codeine (Tylenol #3). As with most medications, each of these has side effects, and drug holidays are needed to maintain efficacy. If you suffer from RLS or PLM, you should also cut down on caffeine intake in the evening as a preventive measure. Stretching exercises around bedtime may help alleviate the discomfort. A hot bath, leg massages, or a heating pad can also help. Because the disorder is usually worse in the first part of the night, you may want to postpone your bedtime and get an extra hour or two of sleep in the morning. When you travel by plane, ask for an aisle seat so that you can get up and walk around. You can get more information on RLS and PLM from the Restless Legs Syndrome Foundation, Inc., in Raleigh, North Carolina, which publishes a newsletter, *The Night Walkers,* with helpful facts about treatment and support groups for families and individuals suffering from these disorders.

NARCOLEPSY

Narcolepsy is characterized by excessive sleepiness or sudden uncontrollable bouts of sleepiness during activities that may be either quiet or active in nature. The struggle to stay awake occurs every day, regardless of the amount of sleep obtained the previous night. At times, the sleepiness can be so overwhelming that it is felt as a "sleep attack." The individual has essentially no control over the sensation and may fall asleep at inappropriate times or places—during a meeting, a conversation, eating, or even while having sex. Sleep may last 15 or 20 minutes and the person usually wakes up feeling refreshed. Unfortunately, this alertness is only short-lived, as the person begins to feel sleepy again within the next 2 to 3 hours. The pattern repeats itself several times a day.

Other symptoms of this disorder are: (1) cataplexy, a sudden muscle weakness that is triggered by intense emotions—fear, anger, excitement, or by laughter, (2) sleep paralysis, an inability to move one's body or limbs during the transition period of falling asleep or waking up, (3) hypnagogic hallucinations, strange and often frightening visual, auditory, or tactile sensations that occur while one is falling asleep or waking. These dreamlike experiences are often difficult to distinguish from reality. Sleep paralysis and hallucinations can occur together, resulting in a frightening experience. Cataplectic episodes may range from muscle weakness to a total physical collapse lasting several minutes.

Sleep scientists do not know the cause of narcolepsy. It is a genetic disorder, presumably linked to a defect of some brain chemicals. Its onset may occur when the patient is 10 to 30 years old, although some people remain undiagnosed until much later in life. Not everyone with narcolepsy experiences all the symptoms described above. In addition, sleep paralysis, also running in families, can be an isolated phenomenon that is not necessarily indicative of narcolepsy. The consequences of narcolepsy vary with the severity of the disorder. As it becomes more severe, it can have a profound impact on an individual's professional, social, and family life. Falling asleep at inappropriate times can be more than a social embarrassment; it can interfere with learning in schoolchildren and jeopardize adults' jobs. Recurrent napping in the evening can put a strain on a marital relationship. Falling asleep unexpectedly at the wheel or while performing a hazardous task can have serious consequences for an individual's life and on public safety.

If you have symptoms of narcolepsy, see a neurologist or a sleep specialist who can evaluate your symptoms and perform sleep studies to make a proper diagnosis. Although there is no known cure for narcolepsy, several medications help to control the symptoms. Stimulant medications are used to treat excessive sleepiness, and some antidepressant medications are helpful in controlling the symptoms of cataplexy, sleep paralysis, and hallucinations. Taking short naps at strategic times during the day helps to alleviate the sleepiness. Because nighttime sleep is disrupted in narcoleptic patients, keeping a regular sleep schedule is also important. The American Narcolepsy Association can provide useful information about new research findings and about support groups for patients and their families.

PARASOMNIAS

The term parasomnia refers to a wide range of unusual, disruptive, or abnormal events that occur predominantly during sleep or during the transitional period from wakefulness to sleep. They may range from simple body rocking as a child falls asleep, to teeth grinding, to painful sleep-related erections, to sleep-related seizures. We review here only some of the most common parasomnias: nightmares, sleep terrors, sleepwalking, eating while asleep, and REM-sleep behavior disorder. Parasomnias do not necessarily lead to a complaint of insomnia or hypersomnia, though in severe forms either of these difficulties may be present. In many cases, they are simply undesirable phenomena. Some parasomnias, however, may cause physical injuries (sleepwalking) and significant psychological distress (night terror) to the person suffering from the condition or to the parents or spouses who witness the episodes.

Nightmares

Nightmares are frightening dreams that occur during REM sleep. They usually depict a story, with vivid imagery of impending danger, in scenes of chasing, falling, or even killing; these may be accompanied by some utterances or screams. Because the body is paralyzed during REM sleep, there is often a sense of being trapped, with no way out. The nightmare typically leads to full awakening, during which there is vivid recall of the dream. The person becomes oriented and alert quickly, although emotional distress and anxiety can interfere with his or her ability to return to sleep. Nightmares are more common in the second half of the night, when REM sleep is predominant. An occasional nightmare is normal in both children and adults. About 5 percent of the general population are troubled by frequent nightmares, and they are common among those who have suffered or witnessed traumatic events—sexual or physical abuse, natural disasters, war and combat experiences. Excessive anxiety and stress can be both cause and consequence of recurrent nightmares. Temporary nightmares can be caused by the use of certain beta blockers for hypertension or the withdrawal of some antidepressant medications.

Psychological treatment is often effective in dealing with recurrent nightmares. It involves a combination of gradual exposure to and the rehearsal in writing or in imagination of the frightening dreams. The nightmare sufferer is trained first to record in writing the bad dreams; to rewrite them, changing their course and outcome; and to rehearse the revised version several times a day. Although guidance from a professional therapist may be needed, an excellent book by Drs. Barry

Krakow and Joseph Neidhardt, *Conquering Bad Dreams and Nightmares,* provides a detailed self-help guide for nightmares sufferers.

Sleep Terror

A sleep terror is characterized by a sudden awakening from deep sleep (stages 3–4) accompanied by a piercing scream, intense fear or anxiety, and excessive autonomic arousal (increased heartbeat, sweating, and agitation). The individual is confused, agitated, and disoriented. During an episode of sleep terror, which may last several minutes, the person is in a mixed state of deep sleep and wakefulness and is unresponsive to other people's efforts to wake her up or calm her down. Children are impossible to console. Unlike nightmares, there is only vague recall or none at all of dreams if the person is awakened from the episode. Often, that is impossible, and he may have no recollection of the incident on arising in the morning. Sleep terrors occur mostly in the first third of the night, when deep sleep is predominant. They are most common among children between the ages of 4 and 12, and the condition tends to resolve itself spontaneously during adolescence. More rarely, it persists or even begins during adulthood.

Sleepwalking

Sleepwalking, or somnambulism, may consist of simply sitting up in bed or getting out of bed and walking around the bedroom; rarely, it may involve walking out of the bedroom and going to another part of the house and even outside the house. Sleepwalkers may carry on conversations that are difficult to understand or that make little sense. They are unresponsive to the efforts of others to communicate with them or to wake them. Full awakening is achieved only through persistent effort, and there is usually confusion, disorientation, and no recall of the incident upon awakening at night or the next morning. The sleepwalker may wake spontaneously during the incident or, more typically, return to bed or awake in the morning in a different room of the house. Sleepwalking and sleep terror have several features in common and often occur together. Sometimes the person will run out of the bedroom or even out of the house in a state of panic, hurting himself along the way. Sleepwalking is more likely to occur in the early part of the night, when deep sleep is predominant. As with night terrors, sleepwalking is more prevalent during childhood and is usually, but not always, outgrown by adolescence.

The causes of sleep terror and sleepwalking are still unclear. The consequences can be serious. Trying to console a child experiencing a sleep terror is extremely distressing to parents, more so than to the child himself. Sleepwalkers are usually good targets for jokes, but there is also significant risk of injuries and legal complications. David, a teenager who was seen in our clinic for sleepwalking, had cut his right arm badly when trying to get out of the house through his bedroom window. Bob, a successful salesperson, found himself, in his underwear, locked out of his hotel room in the middle of the night while on a business trip. A recent highly publicized murder case involved a man who reportedly drove his car 10 miles from his house, killed a relative, and returned to his bed without recollecting the incident. The man was acquitted.

There are several options for treating sleepwalking and sleep terrors. First, if you are parents of children with these disorders, keep in mind that the conditions have a developmental course and are usually outgrown by late adolescence. You should intervene only to prevent injury and minimize sleep disruption. In both children and adults, it is best not to force wakings, but instead to provide reassurance, verbal instructions, and physical guidance in returning the person to bed. Because sleepwalking can lead to injuries, the following safety measures should be taken: the person should sleep on the ground floor; bedroom windows and doors should be locked; all potentially dangerous objects, including weapons, should be removed; furniture should be rearranged to avoid hazards. It is also important to maintain a regular sleep schedule and avoid sleep deprivation. This preventive measure is important because both sleep terror and sleepwalking originate from deep sleep, which is present in a greater amount after a person has been deprived of sleep. When stressful life events or other psychological problems are present, appropriate psychological interventions and stress-management may be useful. Medications suppressing deep sleep can be helpful on a temporary basis to minimize the occurrence at times of stress or sleep deprivation.

Nocturnal Eating Syndrome

This condition is characterized by nighttime wakings, with the person's inability to return to sleep without eating or drinking. Quite common in infants, the condition is not necessarily a sleep disorder, because parents are willing to get up and feed the child. Dr. Carlos Schenck and his colleagues at the University of Minnesota have recently identified a similar condition in adults; the distinctive feature is that nocturnal eating is part of a sleepwalking episode. The sleep eater gets up in the middle of the night and, in a state of partial awakening, prepares, even cooks food and eats it. The behavior is unconscious and the sleep eater has no recollection of the episode the next day.

When I saw Diane, a 45-year-old woman, in our clinic two years ago, she described a classic picture of the nocturnal eating syndrome. Her overt problem was that of sleepwalking, which had been going on for several years, with an average occurrence of 3 or 4 times a week. Typically, though, she would get up in the first half of the night and sleepwalk to the kitchen, engage in an elaborate cooking ritual and bingelike episode, and return to her bed, with no recollection of the incident the next morning. Although these episodes had been witnessed with dismay by her husband and children, usually the only clue was the dirty dishes found in the kitchen the next morning. On some occasions, though, she had left the stove on, and one time the fire alarm went off. Interestingly, Diane had a previous history of a compulsive eating disorder, although at the time of her evaluation in our center she maintained that it was no longer a problem. Whether this nocturnal eating syndrome was an unconscious manifestation of her eating disorder remained unclear.

Aside from weight gain, the consequences of this unusual sleep behavior can be dangerous, as some people cut or burn themselves while preparing food. The exact causes of the disorder, which is more likely to affect women, are unknown. Excessive stress and sleep deprivation can trigger sleepwalking and perhaps this nocturnal eating syndrome. Medication may decrease the frequency of occurrences, and preventive measures are essential. Removing dangerous objects, perhaps even disconnecting the stove or setting up an alarm system to go off should the stove be turned on at night, can prevent a potential disaster.

The condition should be distinguished from nighttime wakings that have become conditioned to hunger; for some people, eating at night is almost an obsession. An individual with an eating disorder like bulimia may engage in a binge at night. In such a case, however, the person eating in the middle of the night, whether by choice or by compulsion, is usually aware of doing so, whereas in the classic nocturnal eating syndrome the person is apparently unconscious.

REM-Sleep Behavior Disorder

This condition is characterized by abrupt and often violent behavior during sleep—punching, kicking, thrashing about, and even falling out of bed. Such behavior occurs mainly during REM sleep, when the body is supposedly paralyzed. This paralysis is at least partially absent in individuals who suffer from REM-sleep behavior disorder, mostly middle-aged and older men. They may be acting out some of their dreams, and there may be emotionally charged verbalizations consistent with their dreams. When a person wakes from such an episode, he is usually alert, coherent, and reports dream content consistent with his behavior. This disorder can be potentially dangerous to the person who suffers from it as well as to the bedpartner. I have seen a case where a retired designer and avid hunter, dreaming he was chased by a grizzly bear, ran into the dresser and broke his foot. Another man, a retired army veteran, woke up from a vivid dream about fighting with the enemy to find his hands around his wife's neck.

Medication such as clonazepam has been found effective in suppressing these episodes. Appropriate safety and preventive measures should also be taken to secure a safer sleep environment and to prevent physical injuries. The person should sleep on the ground floor; night tables, bedside dressers, lamps, or any dangerous objects near the bed or in the bedroom should be removed; and weapons should be put out of reach. Depending on the frequency and severity of those episodes, a spouse may need to sleep in a separate bedroom until the disorder is brought under control with drug treatment.

In this chapter we have reviewed a variety of sleep disorders commonly evaluated and treated by sleep professionals. The conditions represent only a small sample of the more than 80 disorders now recognized in the *International Classification of Sleep Disorders*. They range from simple annoyances, to bizarre or unusual behaviors, to psychologically distressing and potentially life-threatening disorders. If you recognize symptoms of these disorders, you should see a sleep specialist for a thorough evaluation. Sleep-laboratory testing is often required for a proper diagnosis and the most appropriate treatment.

13

Sleep in Children

Most parents would attest to the fact that no child is immune from sleeping difficulties. At one time or another, all children experience disturbed sleep, be it a missed daytime nap or problems falling asleep at night, waking at night, or waking too early in the morning. Occasional episodes of disturbed sleep in children can be caused by illness and fever, the side effects of medication, changes in sleep schedules, pain from teething, or excitement over upcoming pleasurable events or visitors. For most children, disturbed sleep is the exception, and parents are able to adapt to the occasional night of interrupted sleep.

NORMAL SLEEP
Newborns

What is considered "normal" sleep varies with your child's age. Newborns have not yet developed an internal biological clock that tells them when to be awake and when to sleep, so your newborn will not sleep according to your schedule or "the clock" and will have no awareness of daytime and nighttime. Typically, a newborn sleeps 15 to 18 hours a day in short stretches of 2 to 4 hours each, and it is unrealistic for parents to expect the infant to sleep through the night. Instead, you will need to adapt yourself to your child's schedule, sleeping when he sleeps and enjoying him when he is awake. Most newborns can sleep anywhere, since they have not yet learned to distinguish themselves from their environment and are not sensitized to external events. At this point it is OK to have your baby sleep in a crib or bassinet in your room if you wish; you'll be near when he cries at night. A word of warning, though. Some parents become overly anxious with the baby in their bedroom, especially a first child. If you feel compelled to check on your newborn throughout the night or are awakened by the tiny squeaks he makes while sleeping, you should move the baby into his own bedroom after a few nights.

Six to Twelve Weeks

At about 6 weeks (or 6 weeks after the expected delivery date for premature babies) your child's sleep will begin to be more organized, and the sleep periods at night may be up to 6 hours long. After several weeks of having your baby wake every few hours for a feeding, this stretch of uninterrupted sleep will seem like a gift. Your baby will also begin to develop a greater awareness of her world and may begin to fight sleep, preferring to stay awake to interact with you. By 6 weeks you should begin to establish healthy sleep habits in your baby. Since she will now begin noticing her environment, it is important to get her used to sleeping in her own bed. Babies become easily fatigued, and your child may become fussy when she's tired, as her nervous system still lacks inhibitory control. This control will develop as she matures. Put your baby down in her crib after every 2 or so hours of wakefulness. If she stays awake longer, she may become overtired. Avoid having bright colors in the bedroom, and remove such distractions as noises, lights, or toys in the crib that can be overstimulating for your little one.

Three to Six Months

By 3 to 4 months, your child's biological rhythms should be evolving, and a regular sleep-wake cycle should be fairly developed. However, naps may still be irregular as he struggles to establish a daytime sleep-wake cycle. It is important to adjust your caretaking activities to the child's biological needs. Because your child is becoming more socially aware, he may fight sleep in order to play, so try to safeguard his sleep by looking for signs of tiredness, like his rubbing his eyes, pulling on his ear, or increased fussiness. If he misses his naps, he may become overtired and not able to fall asleep, and may have more frequent nighttime awakenings. According to Dr. Richard Ferber, a child sleep specialist at Children's Hospital in Boston, most healthy full-term infants should sleep through the night by the time they are 3 to 4 months old, and by 6 months, all healthy babies can do so.

Six to Twelve Months

Most children between 6 and 12 months go to bed between 7:00 and 9:00 P.M. and wake between 5:00 and 7:00 A.M. Although some babies may still wake at night for a feeding, this is considered to be learned behavior, as there is no nutritional need for a night feeding at this age. Most 6- to 12-month-olds take two naps a day, one in the morning and one in the early afternoon, generally 1 to 2 hours each. If naps are less than 45 minutes they may not be restorative for your baby. Optimal time between naps is 2 to 3 hours. Your child may fight sleep, and if he thinks he can outlast you, he may protest for long periods of time. It is best to put him down for a nap before he becomes overtired or sets off a screaming battle. He may begin to wake at night during this time even though he was a good sleeper before. This may be due to greater daytime physical and mental activity. Putting your baby to bed 30 minutes to an hour earlier may obviate these night awakenings.

Twelve to Thirty-six Months

Between 1 and 3 years, most children sleep an average of 12 to 14 hours in a 24-hour period. Somewhere during this time your child may decrease his naps from 2 to 1. However, there may be a period where 2 naps are too much for your baby and 1 nap isn't enough. A nap at midday or right after lunch may be the best time. Many parents switch their baby to a regular bed during this period. The move may initially cause your child to begin waking up at night again, but if you keep him in his new bed instead of putting him back in his crib or picking him up when he cries, he will soon adapt and sleep through the night. Later in this chapter we'll discuss ways to deal with children who will not stay in their beds at night. The transition to a new bed can be eased if you move along familiar objects, blankets, and toys.

Three Years to Six Years

Most children in this age range go to sleep between 8:00 and 9:00 P.M. and wake up between 6:30 and 8:00 A.M. Naps generally decrease in length, and only about 50 percent of children between 3 and 5 years old nap on a regular basis. During preschool years, children may wake at night with "bad dreams" or nightmares and may be afraid of "things that go bump in the night." That's because children of this age have difficulty distinguishing between fantasy and reality. The average number of night awakenings in a 5-year-old is once a week, though a small percentage of children wake on a nightly basis. Most sleeping problems in children 3 to 6 years old develop as a result of parental inconsistency or negligence in establishing good sleeping habits. Such is the case with the child who repeatedly gets out of bed for one more kiss or drink of water.

Seven Years Through Twelve Years

Although your child will probably argue for a later and later bedtime as she matures, she will still need about 9 to 10 hours of sleep a night to feel alert and to function well during the day. Bedtime problems may also be related to fear of the dark or fear of monsters in the closet or under the bed. Nighttime fears are the most common type experienced by children. More will be said later on how to deal with them.

Adolescence

Adolescents need as much or more sleep than younger children do because of the physiological, cognitive, and social requirements of puberty. Teenagers, however, often become sleep deprived due to social pressure, homework, and extracurricular activities. One study revealed chronic sleep deficits in 13 percent of teenagers. Teenagers may also get their sleep schedules out of whack by shifting their bedtime later and then trying to sleep longer in the morning. One 14-year-old boy named Aaron came to our clinic at the urging of his mother. Aaron typically watched TV until between 2:00 A.M. and 4:00 A.M. and finally fell asleep close to morning. When his mother tried to rouse him for school, he would become belligerent toward her. After about an hour battle, often ending with his mother throwing water on him, Aaron would finally get out of bed. His grades were dropping, as he was continually falling asleep in class. He perpetuated the problem by taking a lengthy nap after school, resulting in his not feeling tired until 2:00 or 4:00 A.M.

DISTURBED SLEEP

Surveys indicate that approximately 20 to 25 percent of children between the ages of 1 and 5 will develop some sleep problems. These children may refuse to nap during the daytime or struggle to avoid going to bed at night. They may require long periods of parental interaction, nursing or being rocked or cuddled before they can fall asleep. Some of these young ones never fall asleep in their own crib or bed but instead fall asleep in a parent's arms, in another room, or in their parents' bed. Other children may wake after a short period of sleep or several times during the night and cry frantically until a parent comes into the rooms to soothe them back to sleep. Often, these children simply haven't learned to fall asleep or return to sleep on their own without being held, rocked, or fed.

What Problems Can Result from Poor Sleep in Childhood?

Sleep can become a nightly "nightmare" for the parents and siblings of poor sleepers, and the consequences for the sleep-deprived child are numerous. In addition to increased daytime fatigue and irritability, the child may also develop learning problems. Many studies indicate that there is a relationship between sleep duration and the child's ability to learn and that a longer sleep duration in babies is related to an increased attention span. Three-year-olds who nap are more adaptable and can adjust to new circumstances better than children who do not nap. When sleep disruption becomes a nightly problem, parents and siblings may also become sleep deprived. Parents, resentful of the child having the sleeping problem, may take out their irritability on the other children. They may restrict their social life in an effort to catch up on their sleep when the child is sleeping; they may fear that a baby sitter will not be able to put the child to sleep. Having become slaves to their child's sleep schedule, they may even experience marital friction as a result of their stress and their conflicting views on how to resolve the problem.

Will My Child Outgrow His Problem Falling Asleep or Waking at Night?

Experts in children's sleep, like Dr. Marc Weissbluth of the Sleep Disorders Center at the Children's Memorial Hospital in Chicago, maintain that most children do not "outgrow" their sleeping difficulties but, rather, require special assistance in establishing good sleep habits. The problems do not magically disappear as the child gets older. Longitudinal studies show that the sleep problems of over 80 percent of all children who are poor sleepers do not resolve themselves spontaneously. Learning to fall asleep unassisted or to soothe oneself back to sleep if one wakes at night is an acquired skill that parents must teach the child.

Teaching Your Child Good Sleep Habits

If your child is 4 months of age or older and is unable to fall asleep on her own or wakes at night and can't fall back to sleep without your help, you may be preventing her from learning an important skill, that of being able to soothe herself to sleep. As we have seen, the lack of this skill can result in sleep deprivation for her as well as for the whole family. The good news is that the skill can be taught, despite months or even years of poor sleep habits.

Keep your child on a regular schedule. Begin by setting a regular bedtime, determined by the child's age and biological clock. The bedtime should correspond with the time your child normally gets sleepy or falls asleep. Try to keep wake-up times, naps, and mealtimes regular and to establish a consistent sleep-wake rhythm.

Establish a bedtime routine and rituals. Develop a regular and relaxing bedtime routine about 20 to 30 minutes before bedtime. This routine may involve bathing and changing the baby for sleep, then nursing or feeding, and rocking or singing to him. For an older child the bedtime ritual may involve a bath, brushing teeth, the reading of a story, or other quiet play. The same ritual should take place every night at around the same time.

Be consistent in the way you put your child to bed. At the end of the bedtime ritual, place your baby in her crib or bed in her room. Bedroom conditions should be the same at bedtime as they will be for the remainder of the night. Kiss and hug her good night and tell her it is time to go to sleep. Then leave the room.

Let your child learn to fall asleep alone. It is important that your child remain awake until bedtime rather than falling asleep in your arms or a place other than her bed. Do not remain in her room until she falls asleep. If she gets used to having you in her room when she falls asleep, you can expect her to cry if you leave before.

From this point on there are two ways to handle your child's behavior. In the "cold turkey method," you walk out of your child's room and do not return until morning. If your child wakes during the night, you do not go into his room. Although this method will ultimately be the quickest and most effective at teaching your child to fall asleep on his own, it is often the most difficult for both the child and the parents. Some parents are unable to tolerate hearing their child scream. And scream he will! He will try just about anything to get you back into the room to soothe and comfort him. In addition to crying, he may rock, bang his head, and throw toys out of the crib. It is important before putting your child to bed to remove any articles that may be dangerous or easily broken.

If you find yourself unable to tolerate his crying or negative behavior, try the progressive approach known as the "gradual extinction method"; it may be more acceptable and less traumatic. If your child cries after you leave his room, go in to check on him after five minutes. Make this check as brief as possible, no more than 1 to 2 minutes long. Do not begin a prolonged interaction with your child and do not pick him up. Simply make sure he is safe and tell him again it is time to go to sleep. Then leave the room. Remember, the goal is to help your child fall asleep alone. If your child continues to cry, wait 10 minutes this time to check him. After that, check him every 15 minutes if his crying persists. When he is quiet or whimpering softly, do not go into the room, as he may be ready to fall asleep and a visit from you will rouse him and start the crying again. Use the same process during the night if he wakes and cries for you. On the second night, you should wait 10 minutes before your first trip to the bedroom, and then 15 minutes, and 20 minutes. If you find the intervals too long, you can shorten them, but only as long as you make them progressively longer. If you go in too quickly, you will only prolong the problem.

Although the gradual extinction method may be more acceptable to you, remember that any trips into your child's room will increase his crying and other behavior geared toward getting you to soothe him or play with him. Breaking your child of such behavior will be more difficult than in the cold turkey method, because he is learning that you will come to him after a certain interval of time. You may find that he can cry for long periods of time until you again come to check on him. That is why, if you are using the gradual extinction method, you must be absolutely consistent about not interacting with your child at this time. Although a quick pat on the back or a little hug may seem innocuous to you, it will serve as a powerful reinforcer of his crying.

How Long Will It Take for My Baby to Learn to Fall Asleep on His Own?

When parents are consistent about not reinforcing their children's crying at bedtime or during the night, most children learn to soothe themselves back to sleep in only a few nights, usually between 3 and 5 nights. Some children will continue to wake and cry but will fall asleep after a short time. For a small percentage of children, the process may take up to 2 weeks. Expect the first night to be the worst. Children will typically cry for 1 to 2 hours the first night, although some may cry off and on the whole night. The second night will probably bring a reduction in the amount of time the child spends awake crying. For parents who work during the week, a Friday night may be the best time to begin the training so that they can nap the next day to make up for some of the lost sleep. One helpful suggestion is to keep a record of your child's crying time. Record the time he is put to bed and how long he cries. If you are using the gradual extinction method, record how many times you checked on him. Also record any times the child woke after initially falling asleep and how long he cried and how many times you checked on him. Do this on a nightly basis so that you can compare nights to see whether your child's crying time is decreasing. If it is not, examine the consistency of your own behavior to see whether you may be perpetuating his crying.

Bedtime Struggles

What should I do if my child will not stay in bed? Children will sometimes test the limits by getting up after being put to bed for the night. They may get up for another drink of water, a hug from their parents, or a request to sleep in their parents' bed. You can teach your child to stay in bed at night. First, you must be consistent about not reinforcing this behavior. If you give in and allow him to get out of bed when he can't sleep at night, you will find that this behavior will become more frequent. Second, you must take your child back to bed every time he gets out of it. This may be wearing on parents, as some children attempt to get up dozens of times a night. When you take your child back to bed, do it quickly and with no discussion, arguments, soothing, or punishment. Make as little eye contact with him as possible. If he repeatedly gets out of bed after having been brought back to his bedroom you may even have to hold the door closed until he is in bed and stays in bed.

To eliminate bedtime struggles, it is also important to reinforce the target behavior, that of staying in bed. You may want to reward the child in the morning with a small gift, a treat, or a favorite activity if he stays in bed all night long. Another technique is to make a chart and give him a star or happy face for each period or block of time he stays in bed. When he accumulates a specified number of stars or faces, he can exchange them for a promised reward or privilege. It is important to give your child praise as well as tangible rewards. Eventually, as your child learns to stay in bed at night, you will want to phase out the material items.

Nighttime Fears

How should I deal with my child's nighttime fears? Your child may go through a period in which she is afraid to go to bed or stay in bed. She may refuse to go to sleep unless her door is open or her light is on. At other times, she may jump out of bed, screaming that something is under the bed, in the closet, or at the window. Scary scenes from movies may replay themselves in her head at night. Regardless of the fear, it is important to teach your child to face and overcome it instead of escaping it by sleeping in your bed or with another family member. Avoidance serves to strengthen fear rather than weaken it and will only reinforce your child's belief that she can't rely on her own resources. Several tactics are effective in dealing with children's nighttime fears.

The first technique, known as self-control training, involves teaching your child adaptive verbalizations to help combat the fearful statements she is already telling herself. You begin by saying the verbalizations aloud. For example, you might say, "Relax. Take a few deep breaths. I'm OK. I'm brave and strong and nothing is going to hurt me. Look at that shadow on the wall. It's only a shadow. I can touch it and there will be nothing there. It's not a monster after all. It's only a shadow from the light shining on my stuffed animal. I'm OK now. I'm very brave." Next, have your child perform the actions—relaxing and taking deep breaths—while you instruct her aloud. Then have her perform the actions again while saying the words aloud. Repeat twice: the first time she whispers the words to herself, and the second time she thinks them but does not speak them.

For recurrent fears, a good technique calls for gradually getting your child used to the feared situation. For example, if he is afraid of the dark, gradually reduce the light in his room on consecutive nights. Installing a rheostat on the light switch can be helpful. Similarly, you can close a door more and more, by small amounts. If the fear is persistent, try other things during the day to desensitize him to the feared stimuli. You might ask your child to draw a picture of what he is afraid of or to act out a scene where he encounters and combats it.

When Eric, at the age of 4, had recurring fears about a gremlin after watching a movie, his mother asked him to draw a picture of the gremlin. Doing so did not help until she came up with the idea of having him draw a cage to put it in. After that, he didn't worry about gremlins at night anymore. A more preventive measure to nighttime fears is to screen your child's TV viewing in order to eliminate images that will wreak havoc on his sleep at night.

What About a Family Bed?

Many parents allow one or all of their children to sleep in their bed each night for all or part of the night. Parents justify this practice because of its convenience for night feedings or care of sick children or because of the belief that it results in emotional bonding between family members. The problem with the family bed is that it may result in sleep deprivation for everyone. If sleeping conditions are too crowded, no one will sleep well. Eventually, as the child gets older, parents will want the child to begin sleeping in his own bed, but once the pattern has been established, it will be hard to break. Your child will have great difficulty sleeping on his own. Parents should be aware of these consequences before they begin letting the child sleep in their bed, no matter how convenient it seems at the time.

Dana was asked by some good friends to take care of their two children, ages 2 and 4, for the weekend. They mentioned that the children sometimes woke at night. That was an understatement! Several times on each of the two nights the children woke and came into Dana's bedroom with the request to get into bed with her. Each time, she promptly took the children back to their room and tried to soothe them back to sleep. At the end of an exhausting weekend the parents returned and informed Dana that the children had never slept through the night in their own bed; they always went into the parents' bedroom to sleep. The father would get out of bed and go to the children's room to sleep. When Dana asked why they hadn't informed her of this pattern, the mother responded that she thought they might sleep through the night in a strange house!

There are important cultural differences in people's beliefs about having children sleep in the same bed as parents. It is a more frequent practice in Asia than in North America. Some people may have a family bed because of space limitations. For parents who like the idea of a family bed as a way of establishing closeness with their children, it is best to allow your children to come into your bed in the morning after you've all had a good night's sleep. Cuddling your little ones in bed is a joy you may not want to miss out on, but do it at a time when it will not instill a bad habit that will someday need to be broken.

OTHER CHILDHOOD SLEEP DISORDERS
Narcolepsy

Narcolepsy (see Chapter 12) is characterized by excessive daytime sleepiness or sudden bouts of sleepiness during daytime activities. There are several other symptoms of this disorder: (1) cataplexy, a sudden muscle weakness that is triggered by intense feelings of anger or excitement or by laughter, (2) sleep paralysis, an inability to move one's body or limbs when transiting from a waking to sleeping state or vice versa, and (3) hypnagogic hallucinations, strange visual or auditory experiences that occur between sleep and wakefulness. The onset of narcolepsy generally does not occur until late adolescence and it is rarely diagnosed in preteens. Unless it is properly diagnosed and treated, narcolepsy can cause learning problems in school. Because of the recurrent and uncontrollable sleep episodes, some children may also be labeled as lazy. There is no cure for narcolepsy, but treatment generally involves a combination of medication and scheduled naps.

Snoring and Sleep Apnea

Although all children snore occasionally as a result of colds or allergies, about 10 to 20 percent of children are habitual snorers. Children who snore have difficulty maintaining a prolonged, consolidated sleep state. They wake frequently and cry out in the night. Snoring is related to another condition known as obstructive sleep apnea (OSA), which is caused by obstruction to the upper airway during sleep, resulting in either partial or total momentary lapses of breathing. These apneic episodes cause frequent nocturnal arousals that can result in excessive daytime sleepiness. Children who have this disorder may exhibit, in addition to daytime sleepiness, mouth breathing, difficulty in swallowing, or poor speech articulation. OSA is more common in boys than in girls, and the average age of diagnosis in children is 7 years. For children with OSA, the most common treatment involves a tonsillectomy or adenoidectomy to remove the airway obstructions. Other forms of treatment are described in Chapter 12.

Sleepwalking

About 10 to 15 percent of children between the ages of 6 and 15 will have occasional episodes of sleepwalking, and about 5 percent will sleepwalk up to 15 times per year. The sleepwalker may sit up in bed, walk around the house, eat, or go outdoors. Sleepwalking usually occurs during the first third of the night, when deep sleep is predominant, and is more frequent during periods of sleep deprivation, illness, or fever, and when certain medications are being used. If your child sleepwalks, the most important thing is to ensure his safety. Remove toys, furniture, or other items from his path. Secure windows and lock doors to the outside. You may gently lead him back to bed and tuck him in. Do not become overly concerned. Sleepwalking that starts before the age of 10 is typically not associated with any emotional, personality, or behavioral problems and will most likely be outgrown with maturation.

Sleep Terrors

Has your child ever let out a piercing scream during the night and sat up in bed with his eyes open and unfocused? If so, he was probably having a night terror. Other symptoms of night terrors include sweating, a rapid heartbeat, gasping for breath, agitation, and the inability to be consoled. Night terrors differ from nightmares in that they occur during deep sleep rather than during REM or dream sleep. In the morning, the child will probably not remember the episode. Sleep terrors occur in about 5 percent of all children and are most common in boys aged 4 to 12. It is not uncommon for night terrors and sleepwalking to occur together. These two conditions, which tend to run in the family, are considered disorders of impaired arousal. Like sleepwalking, sleep terrors are more frequent with fevers, sleep deprivation, or disturbed sleep schedules, as when the child is on a trip. It is important then to maintain a regular sleep schedule and avoid sleep deprivation. These episodes can be very distressing to parents attempting to console their child. It is best not to force the child to wake, which is often impossible, but instead to give verbal reassurance. If the terror occurs in combination with sleepwalking, provide some verbal instructions and physical guidance in returning the child to bed.

Teeth Grinding

Teeth grinding at night, also known as nocturnal bruxism, occurs in about 11 percent of children between the ages of 3 and 7. Between the ages of 8 and 12, the incidence decreases to around 6 percent. Only about 2 percent of adolescents have the problem. Bruxism may cause dental problems, including abnormal wear of the teeth or periodontal tissue damage. Although there have been few studies of the treatment of bruxism in children, effective procedures among adults with this disorder include biofeedback, the use of prosthetic devices at night to deter teeth grinding, and stress-management techniques.

Nocturnal Enuresis

About 25 percent of 5-year-olds wet their bed at night, 15 percent of boys and 10 percent of girls. By the age of 6, only 10 percent still have a bed-wetting problem, and the figure drops to about 3 percent by the age of 12. By and large, bed-wetting is a developmental problem that almost all children will eventually outgrow. The problem of reduced bladder capacity at night may be caused by such medical factors as reduced production of an antidiuretic hormone, urinary tract infection, kidney disorder, or epilepsy. Educational factors, such as lack of parental attention to proper toilet training, may also cause bed-wetting. If your child develops a bed-wetting problem after having been dry for a few months, there may be a psychological cause—stress associated with the arrival of a new baby, family conflicts, a separation.

One of the most effective treatments for enuresis is the bell-and-pad system. In this treatment, the child sleeps on a rubber pad that is connected to a bell. When the moisture hits the pad, the bell sounds, waking the child, so the child associates the sensation of a full bladder with the need to wake before the bell rings. Also helpful is a nightly schedule of waking the child to urinate and the control of the amount of fluid intake before bedtime. Drug treatment is usually not recommended for bed-wetting, but a medicine called imipramine can be useful in preventing bed-wetting when a child is visiting friends or going on an overnight trip.

Summing Up

It is normal for children as well as adults to experience an occasional bad night's sleep. Illness, pain, overtiredness, or overexcitement may cause your little one to lose sleep. It is important not to overreact to such infrequent disruptions of sleep and to realize that "this too shall pass." Chronic sleep loss in your child, however, can result in inattentiveness, fussiness, mood changes, and difficulty in learning. Sleep deprivation may also beget further sleep problems as the child becomes overtired and has trouble settling down and soothing himself to sleep. Insomnia, the most common sleep problem in children, is usually the result of bad habits. Well-meaning parents, who pick up their crying baby at night, prevent their child from learning to rely on her own resources to fall asleep and cause her to become sleep deprived. Luckily, this problem can be easily remedied by the following plan: (1) set up a regular bedtime routine for your child, (2) put her down in her own bed to sleep, (3) say good night and then leave the room, allowing your child to fall asleep by herself, (4) do not return to your child's room to pick her up if she cries.

In some cases, parents are unable to resolve their child's sleep problems by themselves. A psychologist or pediatrician may be able to help. At other times, the child's sleep problems may require help from a professional trained in the assessment and treatment of sleep disorders. Symptoms such as excessive daytime sleepiness, snoring, pauses in breathing at night, muscle paralysis or hallucinations during awakening, or loss of muscle tone when emotions are aroused may be related to such disorders as sleep apnea or narcolepsy. A sleep study will be required to diagnose the condition.

Childhood holds many wonders, and we parents want our children to experience the best in life. Sleep is important to our child's health and well-being. We can safeguard our children's sleep by instilling in them sound sleep habits that will continue the rest of their lives.

14

The Golden Years:
Sleep and Aging

Sleep patterns change with age. Like the graying of your hair, wrinkles on your face, and your muscles' loss of strength and flexibility, sleeping in your sixties is not the same as in your twenties. This does not mean that all changes in sleep patterns are normal, however. Some sleep disorders, especially insomnia, increase in the later years of life, and so does the use of sleeping pills. In this final chapter, we try to dispel some common myths about sleep and aging, describe the most common causes of insomnia and other sleep disorders in late life, and outline simple steps you can take to get a restful night's sleep during the retirement years.

NORMAL CHANGES IN SLEEP PATTERNS AS WE GROW OLDER

Aging is the single most important factor that affects our sleep patterns. The most consistent change with aging is in sleep quality, not in sleep duration. For instance, the proportion of time spent in deep sleep (stages 3–4) decreases gradually from about 20 to 25 percent a night during young adulthood to approximately 5 to 10 percent during one's sixties. This deep slumber virtually disappears when one is in the seventies and eighties. Along with these changes, there is an increase in the amount of light or stage 1 sleep. When sleep is lighter, the person is more easily awakened by noise, movements of a bed partner, or by a full bladder. Not surprisingly, the number and duration of wakenings also increase as we get older. It is not unusual for a 65-year-old to wake up between two and five times a night; some of those wakenings may last only a few minutes and not be remembered the next day, while others may last up to 30 minutes.

Table 14.1. SOME COMMON MYTHS ABOUT SLEEP AND AGING

Sleep needs decrease with aging. False. It is the ability to sleep rather than the need for sleep that declines with aging.

Insomnia is an inevitable fact of growing older. False. Aside from the normal age-related changes in sleep patterns, not all seniors suffer from insomnia.

The sleep pattern of a 65-year-old person is the same as a 75-year-old's. False. Sleep gradually changes from infancy to adulthood and from early retirement through the later years of life.

A sleeping pill can restore a youthful sleep pattern. False. No drug can make you sleep as you did in your twenties. If anything, hypnotics can perpetuate insomnia or mask an underlying problem.

Insomnia in late life cannot be changed. False. Nondrug methods effective for treating insomnia in younger people can also help correct or even prevent sleep difficulties in older people.

Contrary to popular belief, the need for sleep does not decline with aging. Rather, it is the ability to sleep uninterruptedly through the night that is impaired. There is a slight reduction in total sleep time, and many older adults may not get much more than 6.5 hours of sleep a night. However, given that napping is a fairly common practice after retirement, when daytime and nighttime sleep are added together, the total amount of sleep in a 24-hour period of a 50-year-old is similar to that of a 65-year-old. Nevertheless, older adults do not sleep as efficiently as younger or even middle-aged people. They need to spend more time in bed to achieve a comparable sleep duration, and some of that time is inevitably spent awake. For example, a 20-year-old without insomnia sleeps on average about 95 percent of the time spent in bed; in contrast, a 70-year-old without insomnia sleeps just over 80 percent of that time. So sleep is not as efficient or as deep in the later part of life as in younger ages. All those changes may explain why complaints of insomnia increase among older people.

The changes take place fairly gradually over the course of life, and occur even in healthy individuals. The degree and speed of these changes may vary from one person to another, with some experiencing more noticeable changes than others. Aside from individual differences, health and lifestyle factors are also important, as we will discuss below. Not sleeping as well, as long, or as deep as you did when young is a fact of life. Just as your running speed, muscle strength and flexibility, and energy level diminish with aging, so does your ability to sleep. Waking up once or twice a night to go to the bathroom and going right back to sleep is normal. Likewise, there is nothing to worry about if you wake up earlier than usual in the morning, with 6.5 or more hours of sleep, and are able to go about your business as usual the next day. These changes are part of the normal aging process.

Insomnia Is Not an Inevitable Fact of Aging

Despite all the normal age-related changes just described, insomnia is not an inevitable fact of aging. For many elderly people, sleep difficulties clearly exceed the expected changes. If you take more than half an hour to fall asleep, are awake for more than half an hour, or wake up at 4:00 in the morning and are unable to go back to sleep, you may very well suffer from insomnia. More than 50 percent of people over 65 express some dissatisfaction with the quality or duration of their sleep, with about 25 percent reporting persistent and troublesome insomnia. The nature of the difficulties changes with age; problems staying asleep through the night or waking too early in the morning are more common than those of falling asleep initially at bedtime, a more frequent complaint in younger people.

Women tend to perceive their sleep patterns as more disturbed than men, and use more sleeping pills as well. Objective recordings of brain-wave activity, however, indicate that the sleep of older men is more impaired than that of aging women. These gender differences may be explained by the higher incidence in men of other sleep disorders, such as sleep apnea and periodic limb movements, conditions that can interfere with sleep without a person's being aware of them.

COMMON CAUSES OF SLEEP PROBLEMS IN LATE LIFE

There are many factors that can explain the greater frequency of sleep disturbances in the later years of life: medical and emotional problems, lifestyle changes associated with retirement, the biological clock's desynchronization.

The pain associated with arthritis and osteoporosis can disrupt sleep, as can some heart conditions and respiratory problems. Several medications used to treat the ailments can cause sleep disruptions as a side effect. Most diuretics cause people to wake up at night to go to the bathroom.

Changes in lifestyle associated with retirement can also increase the risk of sleep disturbances. Surveys show that retired people leading a sedentary life experience more trouble sleeping at night than those who maintain an active life. The golden years are for many people a time to enjoy life, travel, and activities that they never seemed to have enough time for before. Some seniors, however, are ill prepared for retirement. They lack regular activities and daily routines, and some just stay in bed later in the morning, while others nap on and off all day. Some do it to compensate for sleep loss, whereas others enjoy not having to get up so early for once in their lives. Whatever the reason, such strategies often backfire and aggravate sleep difficulties, just as they do in younger people. Keep a regular bedtime and rising time, and do not spend too much time awake in bed. Also, reserve the bed and bedroom for sleep; do not use it as a recreation room or as the place to worry and escape boredom. If you take a nap, keep it short, less than an hour long, and take it before 3:00 in the afternoon.

There is a tendency as people grow older to have a body clock that runs ahead of its time—a phase advance in the biological clock. People want to go to bed earlier, and they wake up earlier than they did in middle age. This might be a welcome change for night owls, but it can interfere with one's sleep schedule and social life. The obligation to maintain a regular rising time for many working years is one of the most important factors keeping the body clock synchronized with the outside world. If, after retirement, a person fails to maintain a fairly regular schedule, the body clock becomes desynchronized, placing the individual at greater risk of disruptions of sleep patterns. Researchers believe that part of this problem is due to a flattening of the normal body temperature fluctuation. In younger people, there is a decline in body temperature around 11:00 P.M. that is strongly linked to the propensity for sleep. But in older people, this decline is much less and tends to occur earlier in the evening, causing a shift in older people's wake-sleep cycles. Whether this is cause or consequence of a changing behavioral routine is still unclear. Nonetheless, experts on sleep and aging find that you can help keep your body clock running smoothly by setting a daily routine, through involvement in social and community activities, learning a new hobby, exercising, or even holding a part-time job. Combined with plenty of exposure to daylight and outdoor activities, all these can help you maintain a consistent rhythm between days and nights and lead to a more satisfying sleep pattern.

Emotional factors such as anxiety and depression can also disrupt sleep at any age. In late life, worries about health, safety, and possible placement in a nursing home can interfere with restful sleep. Sometimes anxiety about sleep itself can turn an age-related phenomenon into an insomnia problem. A retired accountant was concerned about sleeping only 7 hours and waking up once or twice a night for 10 or 15 minutes each time. He said, "I've never been ill, never gone to the hospital, and I just don't understand what is happening to me now." The main problem was that he was confusing normal changes with insomnia. It may be unrealistic to expect to sleep for a solid 8-hour stretch without interruptions. So be careful to keep your expectations realistic.

Several changes in your life circumstances can cause depression in late life—chronic medical problems, loneliness, and the death of a spouse or close friends. All these factors can affect your moods and sleep patterns. Lack of proper planning for retirement can also lead to boredom and even depression. A person who has maintained a success-ful career but has failed to develop other sources of rewards and pleasures may have a hard time adjusting to retirement. Going to bed early in the evening or staying in bed late in the morning out of loneliness or boredom is no way to improve your sleep pattern. Sometimes a person may focus exclusively on sleeplessness and fail to recognize the underlying depression. If you suspect depression may be the culprit, you don't have to suffer. Talk to your family doctor or seek help from a psychologist or psychiatrist.

OTHER SLEEP DISORDERS IN LATE LIFE

Aside from insomnia, there are a number of other sleep disorders that become more pronounced with age. Most of these conditions have been described in Chapter 12, and are reviewed only briefly here. The *restless legs syndrome* is characterized by an unpleasant, creeping sensation in the calves and an irresistible urge to move the legs. It is worse in the evening, particularly around bedtime, and can prevent someone from drifting off to sleep. A related condition, *periodic limb movements,* consists of brief and repetitive leg jerks during sleep. The movements, which sometimes affect the arms as well, may occur 200 to 300 times a night, unknown to the sleeper. They usually cause multiple brief awakenings, not long enough for the person to remember the next day. When the condition is severe, however, a person may feel extremely tired and have to struggle to stay awake through the day. Restless legs and periodic limb movements, which often occur together, may be caused by iron deficiency or poor circulation. Once the disorders are properly diagnosed, your doctor can prescribe a drug called Sinemet, which is quite effective.

Sleep apnea is a breathing disorder in which a person stops breathing periodically throughout the night. An episode begins with a pause in breathing, lasting anywhere from a few seconds up to a minute, followed by a brief awakening and a loud gasping for air. Sleep apnea is usually caused by an obstruction of the air passage, resulting from a collapse of the muscles in the back of the throat during sleep. In older people, the brain mechanisms regulating breathing may be involved as well. The main consequence of the disorder is excessive sleepiness during the day, causing a person to nod on and off all day or virtually fall asleep at inappropriate times or places. Sometimes an older person with sleep apnea may also experience insomnia. The incidence of sleep apnea increases significantly with aging. Among the young and middle-aged, the condition is more prevalent in men. After menopause, women are at about equal risk with men. If you have symptoms of sleep apnea, such as loud snoring, lapses in breathing, and daytime sleepiness, talk to your family doctor or seek professional help directly at a sleep disorders center.

REM-sleep behavior disorder is a condition seen almost exclusively in middle-aged and older men. The disorder consists of violent behaviors—punching, kicking—while a person is asleep. The behaviors arise from REM sleep, the period when dreams typically occur and the body is usually paralyzed. Experts believe that those afflicted by the condition may be acting out their dreams. The violent movements, often accompanied by screaming, can be dangerous to themselves as well as to their bed partners. A drug called clonazepam has been found effective in suppressing the condition. Safety measures should also be taken to prevent injuries (see Chapter 12 for more details).

When the normal aging process is compromised by a deteriorating medical condition such as Alzheimer's disease, sleep disturbances can become particularly severe. Signs of mental impairments are sometimes more severe at night. The older person may wake up confused, disoriented, and wander about inside the house or even outside, incurring significant risk of injuries. Such nighttime sleep problems can also place a heavy burden on caregivers, spouses, or relatives, causing emotional distress and sleep disturbances in them too. In the long run, this can really take its toll and may force the family to place the elderly relative in a nursing care facility. With more advanced stages of Alzheimer's disease, sleep becomes even more disrupted. One study found that the 24-hour sleep-wake patterns of elderly Alzheimer's patients were completely disorganized. Some brief episodes of sleep intruded into every single hour of wakefulness during the day, and every hour of the night was broken by some awakenings.

THE HAZARDS OF SLEEPING PILLS IN SENIORS

People aged 65 or older represent about 13 percent of the American population. However, the majority of drugs for both daytime anxiety

(26 percent) and sleepless nights (40 percent) are prescribed for this segment of the population. Chronic users of sedative and hypnotic drugs tend to be older persons, placing them at greater risk of dependency. Even if sleep problems are more frequent in the later years of life, there is no sleeping pill that can restore a youthful sleep pattern. Older adults should proceed with extreme caution when using sleeping pills. Because of their slower metabolism, they digest the drugs more slowly and are more sensitive to the effects and side effects of the medications. Drowsiness, diminished mental abilities, and the impairment of physical coordination and driving skills are more frequent and more severe in older people. A survey found that older people who take sleeping pills, particularly the long-acting ones, suffer more frequent falls and hip fractures than people of the same age who do not use sleep medications. Another complication of hypnotic drugs is that they can aggravate breathing difficulties in sleep apnea. Also, there is a risk of unwanted interactions with medications taken for other physical problems. Always tell your doctor all the drugs you are taking and ask your pharmacist about side effects and drug interactions.

SLEEP PROBLEMS IN THE ELDERLY CAN BE TREATED EFFECTIVELY

Getting older and not sleeping restfully are facts of life, but persistent and troublesome sleep problems do not have to be endured. Whether you are young, old, or very old, effective treatment methods are available for most sleep disorders.

Over the past 10 years, I have had a special interest in working with elderly people afflicted with insomnia. This interest has grown from the observation that insomnia is an extremely common problem in late life and that, although sleeping pills are often prescribed, most people prefer a nondrug approach or will suffer their sleep difficulties rather than rely on medications.

We have conducted a series of studies on the clinical efficacy of the behavioral treatment methods described in this book. The participants in those studies averaged 67 years of age, and the range varied from 55 to 85 years. Most people had suffered from chronic insomnia, often present for more than 10 years. The treatment program consisted of 8 weekly 1-hour sessions during which participants were taught the different procedures described in previous chapters—restricting time spent in bed, maintaining a regular sleep-wake schedule, and changing erroneous beliefs and attitudes about sleep. During those 2 months, participants kept a daily sleep log, like that provided in Chapter 5.

Before beginning treatment, participants spent an average of 2 to 2.5 hours awake at night and slept about 5.5 hours a night. Thus, in a typical 8-hour night, they spent about 70 percent of that time asleep and 30 percent awake. At the end of the 8-week program, the amount of time awake at night was reduced to about 70 minutes; that is, about 20 minutes to fall asleep, 30 minutes awake in the middle of the night, and 20 minutes awake just before rising time. The increase in total sleep time was modest, about half an hour longer than before treatment. But sleep was more efficient, with seniors sleeping about 82 percent of their time spent in bed. Most participants in the program were satisfied and felt more in control of their sleep patterns. Before the study, more than 50 percent of elderly insomniacs had been using sleeping pills. One year later, only 5 percent had returned to medication.

In another study, we compared the efficacy of this same behavioral approach to a commonly used sleeping pill. We found that although both treatments worked fairly well in the short term, insomnia sufferers who followed the self-management approach fared much better in the long run. In other words, those who learned how to change their sleep habits and schedules, and revised their beliefs and attitudes about sleeplessness, continued to improve their sleep patterns or maintain improvements up to 2 years after completion of the treatment program. In contrast, those who relied on sleeping pills usually returned to the same disturbed sleep pattern after completing treatment.

These findings should be quite encouraging to you or to a relative who suffers from insomnia, even an elderly person. There are many steps you can take to enjoy more restful sleep and a better quality of life. The studies just described involved professional guidance, but you can easily implement the treatment program outlined in this book. As there are many other conditions that can cause insomnia, particularly in older people, you may also seek a professional evaluation of your sleep problem to rule out such causes before you undertake this program on your own.

Much effort and large sums of money are spent in fabricating synthetic substances to slow down the aging process, restore a youthful sleep pattern, and even prolong life. Until such cures are found, you may need to accept the fact that sleep will deteriorate somewhat as you grow older, just as wrinkles will show up over the years. But if you suffer from persistent and troublesome sleeping difficulties that are more severe than those expected from aging alone, the treatment program described in this book can help you get a more restful night's sleep.

Appendix A
List of Helpful Organizations

American Sleep Apnea Association
2025 Pennsylvania Ave. NW
Suite 905
Washington, DC 20006
Phone (202) 293-3650
Fax (202) 293-3656

American Sleep Disorders Association
1610 14th St. NW
Suite 300
Rochester, MN 55901
Phone (507) 287-6006
Fax (507) 287-6008
e-mail asda@millcomm.com

Better Sleep Council
333 Commerce Street
Alexandria, VA 22314
Phone (703) 683-8371
Fax (703) 683-4503

National Foundation for Sleep and Related Disorders in Children
4200 W. Peterson Ave.
Suite 109
Chicago, IL 60646
Phone (708) 368-6799 or
(708) 971-1086

National Institutes of Health
National Center for Sleep Disorders Research
NIHI/NHLBI/NCSDR
Two Rockledge Centre
Suite 7024
6701 Rockledge Dr. MSC 7920
Bethesda, MD 20892-7920

Narcolepsy Network
P.O. Box 1365
FDR Station
New York, NY 10150
Phone (914) 834-2855

National Sleep Foundation
1367 Connecticut Ave. NW
Suite 200
Washington, DC 20036
Phone (202) 785-2300
Fax (202) 785-2880

**Restless Legs Syndrome
Foundation**
304 Glenwood Ave.
Raleigh, NC 27608
Phone (919) 834-0821
Fax (919) 832-4273

**Sleep Disorders Dental
Society**
11676 Perry Hwy #1
Suite 1204
Wexford, PA 15090
Phone (412) 935-0836
Fax (412) 935-0383

Sleep/Wake Disorders Canada
3089 Bathurst St.
Suite 304
Toronto, Ontario
Canada M6A 2A4
Phone (416) 787-5374 National
office
(800) 387-9253 Canada

Index

Charles M. Morin, Ph.D., is Associate Professor of Psychology and Director of the Sleep Disorders Center at Laval University, Quebec, Canada. From 1986 to 1994 he taught at and was the director of the Sleep Disorders Center at the Medical College of Virginia, at Virginia Commonwealth University. Dr. Morin is recognized as a leading authority on insomnia treatment. He has been conducting clinical sleep research and treating patients with insomnia for the past 12 years, and has published extensively and lectured internationally on the topic. He is a Diplomate of the American Board of Sleep Disorders Medicine and a Fellow of the American Psychological Association. In 1995, Dr. Morin was awarded the prestigious Distinguished Scientific Award for an Early Career Contribution to Psychology by the American Psychological Association.